HOCKEY'S
Young
guns

Transcontinental Books
1100 René-Lévesque Boulevard West
24th floor
Montreal (Quebec) H3B 4X9
Tel.: 514 340-3587
Toll-free 1-866-800-2500
www.thehockeynews.com

Bibliothèque et Archives nationales du Québec and Library and Archives Canada
cataloguing in publication

Dixon, Ryan
Hockey's Young Guns : 25 Inside Stories on Making it to the Big Leagues

At head of title: The Hockey News.

1. Hockey players - North America - Anecdotes. 2. Hockey players - North America - Pictorial works. 3. National
Hockey League - Anecdotes. I. Kennedy, Ryan. II. Title. III. Title: Hockey news (Montréal, Québec).

GV848.5.A1D59 2007   796.962'6409227   C2007-941273-4

Project editor: Jason Kay
Project consultant: Arnold Gosewich
Copy Editing: Sam McCaig
Proofreading: Jamie Henderson
Photo research: Matt Filion
Photo credits: Sports Action Photography and Getty Images
Cover design and layout: Studio Andrée Robillard

Printed in Canada
© Transcontinental Books, 2007
Legal deposit — 3rd quarter 2007
National Library of Quebec
National Library of Canada

ISBN 978-0-9738355-5-7

We acknowledge the financial support of our publishing activity by the Government of Canada through
the BPDIP program of the Department of Canadian Heritage, as well as by the Government of Quebec
through the SODEC program Aide à la promotion.

For information on special rates for corporate libraries and wholesale purchases, please call
1-866-800-2500.

The Hockey News

Ryan Dixon and **Ryan Kennedy**

HOCKEY'S Young guns

Transcontinental Books

For Chris

Acknowledgements

Thank you to Jason Kay and Gerald McGroarty for believing a book about young guns could be written by two young guys just getting started in their own careers.

Thank you to every member of *The Hockey News* staff for insights and information regarding how each chapter should be approached and for lending their help in tracking down players for interviews.

Thanks to the players for dusting off old memories and to the extremely cooperative family and friends of these players for sharing stories, digging up old pictures and doing all the things they did along the way to help make their children turn into hockey heroes for a new generation.

Ryan Dixon would like to thank his parents for making sure his minor hockey days were so similar to the ones detailed in this book. He's sorry his stone hands prevented him from paying them back with a million dollar payday, but he hopes this book accounts for something.

Ryan Kennedy would like to thank all his family and friends for their tireless support and willingness to listen to every "fantastic new concept" he comes up with, no matter how ludicrous the idea. Special thanks to his wife, Christine, who has happily committed to a lifetime of hearing about such gonzo schemes.

Foreword

Making the NHL isn't easy.

Young players have to understand that reaching the NHL means making many sacrifices. In the case of most young players, those sacrifices mean getting up at ungodly hours to go to an arena, traveling long distances on a bus and perhaps even leaving home as young as 14 years old.

For whatever reason, passion for the game burns deeply in a hockey player, and those sacrifices don't really seem to matter. It's all about one dream, one goal, one idea—the NHL or bust. And once players realize their dream of making the big time, they become consumed by a single obsession—winning the Stanley Cup.

Working toward obtaining Lord Stanley's Cup is a tremendous goal. The trophy carries all kinds of historical significance, but when the Champagne is being sipped, many of the best stories being told are about the sacrifices players made along the way to reach that euphoric point, and the willingness of their families and friends to lend unconditional support along the way in helping them realize their Cup dream.

Parents get so heavily involved in their children's progress that they become attached to the dream as well. Sometimes, for the lucky ones, the dream ends happily. Other times, not so well. But at the end of it all, hockey forges a bond between parents and children that can be unbelievably strong and mean so much, not just in hockey, but in life as well.

Over the years, I've had a chance to work at many hockey schools, coach many players and see guys realize their dream of making the NHL. I was also a part of two Stanley-Cup-winning teams with the Pittsburgh Penguins: first as an advanced scout on a team coached by the late great Bob Johnson in 1991, then as an assistant coach to the legendary Scotty Bowman in 1992. To feel the Cup in your hands and to take part in what transpires after you win the Cup is an amazing thing—it's an out-of-body experience. That's what young players dream about; that's what the parents of young players dream about. That one moment, that one opportunity, that chance to do the one thing very few people in the history of the game ever get an opportunity to do—win the Stanley Cup.

It's fascinating how people continue to sacrifice and continue to work so hard in the hopes of cracking the NHL. It's a 12-month-a-year commitment now. And anybody who wants to make a career of playing hockey better get used to one word: constant. It's constant training, constant probing, constantly looking for the one thing that will make you better and the one thing that will get you over the top. You're constantly under the microscope. You're constantly working. You're constantly trying to get better.

Just imagine Sidney Crosby and what he has gone through to get to where he is. Not only is Sidney a tremendous player, he's an amazing person. I've spent a lot of time with Sidney, and talked with him often. I'm blown away by the young man's maturity, his focus, his desire and his willingness to do whatever it takes to be better—not just as a player, but as a person.

For all the talk of hard work and sacrifice, it should never be forgotten that, first and foremost, hockey is meant to be fun. Sure, there are pressure points, and sometimes you're going to have to dig a little deeper to find the fun aspects of the game. But they're always there, especially when you're young. Hockey shouldn't be a chore, and if it is, you probably shouldn't be playing. Hockey should be about camaraderie, getting better, enjoying the moment, feeling the speed of the game and utilizing your athletic ability and creative skills to enjoy it as much possible. It shouldn't be difficult. It should be a special experience in your life—something you'll always remember.

The fondest memories I have as a young person growing up in Montreal involve going to the outdoor rinks and playing with my brothers and our friends in non-supervised games where we didn't even keep score—it was always last goal wins. We always wanted to win, but we were having more fun finding out who would get that last goal. It was never about the number of goals scored, it was always about the last one. Sometimes, we'd play just to keep the game going. That's what made it fun.

Every year when I watch young players at the World Junior Championship, I see that same youthful enthusiasm for the game that I felt as a kid. Covering this tournament is one of the real privileges I have had in my career. The world juniors is something that tells players they're on the doorstep of making the NHL. They're that close. For a lot of the players, competing in that tournament—and potentially the gold medal game—may be the summit of their hockey experience. When it's all said and done, they've banked memories they'll never lose, and they'll be bound forever to the teammates with whom they shared that unique experience.

If you're a young player reading this book, recognize the lessons these young men had to learn in order to make it. It'll teach you a lot about what's required to get to the top. Dreams are good, but the only way a dream is fulfilled is if you work to obtain it. Realizing a dream isn't free. It costs in blood, it costs in sweat, it costs in tears, it costs in effort. Every single player you'll read about in this book has worked an amazing amount of time to get to where they are today.

Pierre McGuire

Contents

Introduction

The toughest lesson I've had to learn as the father of two athletically minded and competitive boys is letting go. It's a concept I still find slippery on occasion.

I've had several jarring reminders over the years, times when I've found myself churning inside over a referee's call, a coach's decision, my son's execution. Then, eventually, sanity kicks in when I realize my angst isn't about my offspring, it's about me.

Ditto for the occasions when, on the drive home, I volunteer 'constructive' advice. In the rearview mirror, I can see the eye rolls or the distant looks and I eventually recognize the kids have moved on and aren't interested in how-to-improve seminars.

Fortunately, I now get it more often than not, and I almost always blend into the scenery. I'll watch closely, but I know my place: taxi driver, treat-fetcher, skate-tying guy, role model. If I have any feedback for them, I'll ask if they want to hear it first. If the answer is no, I stash it away.

And I let go of whatever it is I think I want them to be. Because, for that hour on the ice or the field or the diamond, what they really want to be is themselves. Go figure.

The concept of enjoying the experience of being a young hockey player, more than any other notion, is what permeates the chapters in this book. From Mike Richards of the Philadelphia Flyers to Marc-Andre Fleury of the Pittsburgh Penguins, from Dion Phaneuf of the Calgary Flames to Ole-Kristian Tollefsen of the Columbus Blue Jackets, the mantra is repeated: have fun, have fun, have fun.

We hope you have a good time, and learn a few things, while digesting what we have to offer in the ensuing pages. We've identified 25 of the brightest young talents in the NHL and asked them to relate their stories of climbing the ladder to the pinnacle of their profession.

Twenty of the 25 chapters are written by two of *The Hockey News'* young guns, Ryan Kennedy and Ryan Dixon. Five more are contributed by veteran hockey writers. The intention of the book is to illustrate the amount of sweat and sacrifice it takes to reach the top, to provide a road map of sorts for aspiring players looking to improve and get to the next level. If you find a few nuggets that help you in your game, all the better.

But it's also important to remember that our chosen 25 are among the very small minority. Our boys might play in the big leagues, but chances are they won't. Hopefully, they'll be left with memories every bit as warm, and experiences every bit as rich, as the ones who go all the way.

Jason Kay
Editor
The Hockey News

Hockey's Young Guns

Patrice
Bergeron

Taking It All In

Born:	July 24, 1985 – Ancienne-Lorette, Que.
First Team:	Sillery Voiliers
Heroes:	Joe Sakic, Peter Forsberg
NHL Debut:	Oct. 8, 2003 vs. New Jersey

E ventually, Patrice Bergeron's passion for hockey would become glaringly obvious to anybody who watched him play. But those who happened to see Patrice during his first few months on ice could be forgiven if they thought the game wasn't really for him.

Twice a week, Patrice's parents would pack up his equipment and take him to the rink so he could practise skating and learn the game. Initially, it looked like he wasn't cooperating.

"The first time he played at five years old he refused to skate," said Sylvie, Patrice's mom. "He was sitting on the ice in the net. For two days a week and for one hour and a half, when he went on the ice he was on his knees and he would go in the net and stay there, for the whole hour and a half."

This trend continued from September to December.

"Each time we thought, 'This is the last time he'll come, he doesn't like it,' " Sylvie said. "But each time he got off the ice he'd say, 'Wow, I love that.' He just sat in the net and waved at us, blew us kisses with his hand."

Everybody, including his coaches, assumed Patrice had no interest in the finer points of the game. But three months after he first plunked down in the crease, Patrice stood and, to everyone's surprise, started skating quite efficiently around the ice. Turns out some learn by doing, while some learn by watching.

"Everybody thought we went on the ice with him at other times, but no, that was the only time," said Sylvie, emphasizing she was just as shocked as anyone to learn Patrice could not only skate, but skate very well.

Sylvie would soon find out just how much Patrice, now a centre with the Boston Bruins, loved to play and that he also wasn't all that particular about where he and his older brother, Guillame, could start a game.

"His brother was his role model," Sylvie said. "They played in the street, ponds, everywhere they could—even in the house. Hockey sticks were all over the house."

Patrice, who grew up in Sillery, a borough of Quebec City, remembers those days fondly. He also has great memories of his early, organized-hockey days, when his novice team got to play on a very grand stage.

"There's a huge novice tournament in Quebec," Patrice said. "If your team was good enough to get to the final game, you had a chance to go play in Le Colisee. Back then the Nordiques were still playing and it was a big deal for us. We had a good team that year and we went to the final and we won. It was one of my best memories growing up."

Things got even better after Patrice was named player of the game in the deciding contest.

"It was awesome," he recalled. "I had a chance to meet Guy Lafleur after the game and my whole family was there—not just my brother and parents, but also my uncles and grandparents. It was a huge deal for me."

Long before Patrice ever donned a Boston Bruins jersey, he was back at Le Colisee wearing the sweater of his favourite team growing up, the Quebec Nordiques. In 1995, the Nordiques left for Colorado and became the Avalanche. Shortly after the Nordiques left town, Quebec City hosted the 40th edition of its famed international peewee tournament. At the derby, each peewee team represents an NHL club by wearing its jersey. Patrice's team, which consisted of players from Sillery and nearby Sainte-Foy, won the honour of wearing the Nordiques jersey, which was brought back for the special occasion.

As naturally gifted as Patrice was, he still had to overcome some tough obstacles en route to making the NHL.

"I was fairly small when I was growing up. When I was 16, I went to the triple-A midget tryouts and got cut," he said. "It was kind of a big deal to get cut because hockey was huge for me and a big part of my life. But when I got cut, I tried to shake it off and make the best of it in (double-A) bantam."

Patrice's positive attitude and hard work were rewarded. Not only did his bantam team excel, he experienced the personal thrill of being drafted into the Quebec League by the Acadie-Bathurst Titan the following spring.

"I made the best of that year," he said. "We finished third in the whole province of Quebec and I got drafted. It was a good year for me, even though I wasn't thinking that (when I got cut from midget)."

It's no surprise to Sylvie that Patrice showed perseverance. She said her son always embraced the idea of improvement.

"When he was five or six years old, he always worked on his game to be better," she said. "Not to be better compared with other young players, but compared with himself. If he's at point A, he wants to go to point B, C, things like that."

That internal drive and desire to get better is what helped fuel Patrice's early arrival on the NHL scene. After just one full year of major junior, he cracked the Bruins' lineup at the age of 18. Patrice then went on to make national team history. He is the only player to have represented Canada at a World Championship (in 2004) before playing in a World Junior Championship (2005). His efforts helped Canada win gold at both events and Patrice was also named tournament MVP at the world junior tournament.

Looking back, Patrice says one aspect of his practice regimen wasn't much fun as a kid, but it helped get him where he is now.

"I think the one thing I hated most was the power-skating drills," he said. "They take the puck away from you and you just go out there and work on your cross-overs, on your stops and starts, all that stuff.

"I was like, 'Ah man, I need a puck, I want to play,' but at the same time you need to do that to get better, to be a better skater. Especially now with the new rules (in the post-lockout NHL), being a good skater is huge. But you don't realize it when you're young."

Just as Patrice has come to appreciate the not-so-fun aspects of practice, he also now fully realizes how lucky he was to have parents who didn't mind tripping over hockey sticks in the living room or continually taking a son to the rink who, at least initially, did more sitting on the ice than skating.

"My mom and dad, for sure, were as big an influence as my brother was," he said. "I can't say enough about what they've done. I know I'll never be able to thank them enough."

★★ TIP *"Especially when they're young, kids need to be having fun while playing the game. Two things to always work on are your stickhandling skills and your speed. Today's game puts a huge emphasis on speed."*

– Ryan Dixon

Matt
Carle

Northern Star

Born:	Sept. 25, 1984 – Anchorage, Alaska
First Team:	KFC
Heroes:	Brett Hull, Wayne Gretzky, Mike Peluso
NHL Debut:	March 25, 2006 at Minnesota

If there were any doubt as to whether San Jose defenceman Matt Carle had the drive to make it to the NHL, he put it to rest long ago during one car ride home from practice.

Carle, all of six years old, was telling his father which NHL teams he would like to play for in the future, when his dad, Bob, decided to give him a reality check.

"I asked him, 'Do you know how many boys out there have the very same dream and how many of them make it?' He turned to me and said, 'Well, somebody has to make it to the NHL and it may as well be me,' " Bob recalled.

Matt had just begun playing hockey the year before on a team sponsored by his father.

"It was one of those leagues where you just sign up and play," Matt remembered. "The rink I played at was in a mall. It was a small ice surface, which was good because at that age a lot of kids could barely stand up."

Not only could Matt stand up, but in the next few years, he would show everyone he could flat-out play.

Growing up in Anchorage, Alaska, it wasn't enough for Matt to just stand out—he had to stand out, then fly off to faraway tournaments in places like Vancouver or Minnesota and stand out again just so scouts could get a look at him.

"It got pretty expensive," Matt said. "I'm grateful my parents forked over all that money for me."

Of course, all that travel also made for fast friends on the team.

"Three or four of us would share a room," Matt remembered. "You'd sleep in a cot or share beds. I'm still friends with a lot of those guys."

And while Bob went to some tournaments, he couldn't make them all. He wasn't worried, though.

"It was never a problem for me," Bob said. "We missed him, sure, but I knew he could take care of himself. He could cook, he knew how to do laundry, you never had to ask him about his homework—he was self-sufficient."

Matt was also mad about hockey. His heroes growing up included obvious superstars such as Brett Hull and Wayne Gretzky, but also University of Alaska-Anchorage alumnus Mike Peluso. "He was the only guy that kinda went anywhere," Matt said.

Alaska's long, cold winters also provided perfect hockey weather nearly all the time. "Every public school had an outdoor rink that they'd flood in the winter," Matt said. "I'd go over with a couple of buddies and play pick-up all the time and at night they'd put on the floodlights."

One very special person Matt played hockey with was his cousin Brian, younger than Matt by a month. The two were baptized together and played hockey together until Matt's skills took him further, but they remained close. Brian, at 6-foot-6 and 280 pounds, was a big young man. In April 2006, he was working at an excavating company in Anchorage while Matt was making his playoff (and NHL) debut with San Jose. Brian came home from a long, tiring day at work and left a phone message for Matt, telling him how proud he was of his cousin and how much he loved him. Brian then went to sleep, and passed away at the age of 21.

The next day, Matt got Brian's message, followed by a phone call from his parents telling him Brian was gone.

Matt, who had worn No. 25 until Mike Grier joined the Sharks, now wears Brian's old No. 18 as a tribute.

Ironically, it was Brian's older brother, Michael, who first inspired Matt to play hockey—neither of his parents were particularly athletic. Far from a crazed hockey dad, Bob admits it took a while for him to realize just how good his son was.

"I go (to games) because my kid is skating," he said. "But then you start hearing people say 'watch out for that kid,' or 'man, that kid's the best defenceman in Alaska.'"

It also didn't hurt that Matt's passion for the game was off the charts.

"This is a kid who would wake *me* up at six in the morning to go to practice," Bob added. "He was so dedicated."

That dedication landed Matt on the Boston Icemen summer team at the age of 12, the coveted Ann Arbor, Mich.-based U.S. national team development program at 16 and the Omaha, Neb.-based River City Lancers of the United States League. That led to a collegiate career at the University of Denver, which culminated with the Hobey Baker Memorial Award in 2006 as the best player in U.S. college hockey.

Despite all the travel, Bob never considered keeping Matt in Alaska.

"He was like a horse; you gotta let him run," he said.

One story that illustrates Matt Carle's tenacity comes from his days as a bantam player back in Alaska. The team was playing a Christmastime tournament in Vancouver and Matt had made the trip without his parents.

Bob got a call from his son on the Thursday. Matt wasn't feeling well; he was light-headed and wasn't sure if he could play. Bob told him to do what he felt was right, but after the phone call, the team's coaches had come to Matt and pleaded their case: the championship game was that night and they could really use the youngster's skill and leadership.

Ever the trooper, Matt suited up. His team lost the game, but Matt was named MVP. He flew home on Friday and woke up Saturday with no appetite, still feeling sick. Disturbed, Bob took his son to the hospital, where it was revealed Matt had played that championship game with a ruptured spleen. One-third of the blood in his body had leaked into his abdomen and doctors were almost sure they would have to remove his spleen. Matt was taken to the children's intensive care unit; a comical sight once he was out of danger.

"There were airplanes painted on the walls—his feet were hanging off the end of the bed," Bob laughed. "His teammates came to visit him and gave him such crap."

In the end, not only did Matt keep his spleen, but he led his high school team to the championship a month and a half later.

From the isolation of Alaska to the Shark Tank in San Jose, Matt Carle has excelled at all levels. Even when he was sent down to the American League in 2006–07 with teammate Steve Bernier, he learned from the experience.

"It's a long flight from San Jose to Worcester," Matt noted. "Steve and I talked on the flight there and we agreed that the sooner we got over it, the sooner we'd be back in San Jose.

"I learned to lighten up and not put so much pressure on myself. I had been gripping my stick pretty tight, so I just went down there and had some fun."

For Bob Carle, his son's NHL career seems like it was predestined, all the way back to that car ride with a precocious six-year-old.

"It's like when Babe Ruth pointed to the fence and hit the home run," Bob said. "At age six he was pointing at the fence and said, 'Yep, I'm gonna do that.'"

 *"As a defenceman, you can never work on skating too much. We have a power-skating coach in San Jose and it may sound boring, but the same power skating they teach you when you're eight is still important now."*

– Ryan Kennedy

Sidney
Crosby

Emperor Penguin

Born:	Aug. 7, 1987 – Cole Harbour, N.S.
First Team:	Cole Harbour Red Wings
Heroes:	Wayne Gretzky, Mario Lemieux, Steve Yzerman
NHL Debut:	Oct. 5, 2005 at New Jersey

When Sidney Crosby was seven years old, he did his first interview as a hockey player.

"I didn't think anything of it," he recalled. "I just remember my parents telling me some lady wanted to ask me some questions."

Thirteen years later, Sidney has been the focus of every media outlet that covers the sport and a lot of others that usually don't. The Pittsburgh Penguins phenom is the youngest captain in NHL history, the youngest to score 100 points in a season and has already won four major awards (Calder, Art Ross, Hart and Pearson). Coming out of the lockout, his drafting was just the jolt of electricity the moribund league needed.

Sidney grew up in Cole Harbour, N.S. His father, Troy, was a goalie who had been drafted by the Montreal Canadiens. By the time Sidney was two and a half, he and Troy were skating once a week in a parent/tot program. Needless to say, the seed had been planted.

As a child, Sidney's advanced skills often had him playing with kids several years older than he, and his famous drive was already taking form.

"I would play any sport, basically," Sidney said. "I played baseball competitively for a while, but I enjoyed anything that involved competing, and I lived around so many kids, there was always something to do."

"He was always very active," Troy noted. "He wasn't the type to sit in front of the TV."

Troy first realized Sidney's potential early on. "Probably when he was six years old," Troy said. "He was playing with kids three to four years older and excelling."

Sidney would continue to excel as a teenager, but that's when the rules became a barrier. As a 13-year-old, Sidney made the roster of the Dartmouth Subways, a major midget team made up of 16- and 17-year-olds. But Hockey Nova Scotia didn't think having a player so young was appropriate, so he was forced to go back and play for a triple-A bantam team in Cole Harbour. The next year, Sidney went back to the Subways as a 14-year-old and was allowed to stay—and flourish.

"He was competing on an even keel," said Brad Crossley, coach of the Subways. "He was extremely mature beyond his years."

Naturally, Sidney was still the rookie in the room and Crossley recalls the transition.

"In the beginning, he was quiet," Crossley said. "He would sit back and watch guys, learn what it was all about."

Eventually, however, Sidney came out of his shell and started joking around with all the other players. "He had fun," Crossley said. "The guys in the dressing room liked to joke around and he was right in there with them."

On the ice, though, his demeanor never changed. "Intensely competitive," Crossley recalled. "When it came time to play, he was more intense than anyone."

That intensity and skill combined to form a force of nature on the ice that dominated every challenge. Naturally, Crossley saw this talent and made sure to give Sidney the creative license to use his gifts.

"A player like that is special, you just let him go," Crossley said. "We had specific power play set-ups designed for him, but other than that, you just let him play. He was an on-ice general."

For his part, Sidney remembers the impact Crossley had on his career.

"It was a great experience and team," Sidney revealed. "(Crossley) stressed the details and really pushed each guy on and off the ice."

One new wrinkle that all the Subways had to deal with that year was the media presence that followed Sidney to games and tournaments, wherever they went. "It took us a while to get used to, but he was very business-like," Crossley said. "It was not uncommon to have cameras follow him at games. It was pretty intense, but he dealt with the pressure as simply as putting on his skates."

Sidney's official coming-out came at the national championships that year, which were held in nearby Bathurst, N.B. Sid the Kid torched the competition, taking the Subways to the final on the strength of 27 points in six games.

"I don't think that's been matched since," Crossley said. "He carried us. He put that team on his back."

The Subways, however, lost in the final.

That same year, the Crosbys began looking at options for Sidney's future. While playing in a tournament in Calgary, the Subways played Shattuck-St. Mary's, a hockey-driven prep school powerhouse located in Minnesota, with alumni including New Jersey's Zach Parise and Chicago's Jonathan Toews.

"I did some research on the school and was impressed by its program," Troy said. "I thought it would be a good place for him to grow as a player and as a person, to go to school and play hockey at a high level."

Not only did the move take Sidney out of the growing media glare in Atlantic Canada, it also provided him with a top-flight program to hone his skills.

"It was the perfect place for me," Sidney said. "I was playing hockey every day for the first time and was away from home, which made me grow up a little faster. And I was out of the spotlight for a bit and just able to be a kid at school, so it worked out well."

Sidney continued to play well at Shattuck and kept up in his studies, too. "I did well," he said. "I wasn't a brain, but I worked hard and took it seriously. I enjoyed history the most."

Ironic, considering how much history Sidney has already made in his NHL career.

Talk to those close to him and they'll reveal how Sidney really hasn't changed that much since he was a youngster.

"He has always been very determined and dedicated," Troy said. "Really not that different than he is today. Although he has become more recognizable, I don't think of him as a celebrity—he is doing what he has always loved to do."

Crossley still remembers the dazzling array of hockey smarts Sidney brought to his game back then, the same skills he showed off in junior with Rimouski of the Quebec League and in the NHL with the Pens.

"He was always a step ahead, knowing where the puck was going to go and making plays," Crossley said. "He had that vision. He saw the ice like no one else."

For Sidney, the game is still something he is passionate about, the thing that drove him even at a young age.

"I think I knew I had a passion maybe more than others," he said. "I always really enjoyed watching Steve Yzerman. I liked how he played with an edge and was a great leader and did anything it took to win and help his team."

Based on what Sidney has already accomplished in the NHL, it's safe to say he's on the right path.

✦ DRILL   *"Lean a stick against a pylon and stickhandle through it as if it were a defenceman. There are always sticks around in a game and this will help you maneuver through them."*

                                                        – RK

Marc-Andre
Fleury

A Goalie, Not a Statistician

Born:	Nov. 28, 1984 – Sorel, Que.
First Team:	Ninjas of Sorel
Heroes:	Patrick Roy, Martin Brodeur
NHL Debut:	Oct. 10, 2003 vs. Los Angeles

When Marc-Andre Fleury joined the Pittsburgh Penguins he was, in many ways, more one of the boys than one of the men. That created an interesting and fun dressing room dynamic, especially if you happened to be the son of a Penguin.

Marc Bergevin, who had 19 years on Marc-Andre when they roomed together on Pittsburgh road trips during the 2003–04 season, recalled one afternoon when the rookie goalie, still a teenager at the time, quickly transitioned from stopping pucks fired by NHL shooters to stoning pre-teen boys who were whacking balls of tape at him in the dressing room.

"A lot of the guys brought their kids in after we were done showering," said Bergevin of the post-game activities that afternoon. "I was looking for my son and Marc-Andre was playing goalie in the dressing room and all the kids were trying to score on him. I'll never forget that.

"I said (to my son), 'Wes, let's go' and he said, "No, Fleury is the goalie; we're trying to score on him.' "

It sure wasn't tough for kids like Bergevin's son to relate to Marc-Andre. Not only was he very willing to participate in impromptu dressing-room shootouts with them, he also had very little use for shaving cream.

"When they looked at him, even Mario (Lemieux's) little boy Austin, they were always amazed; they're looking at this NHL goalie, this superstar in the making, and he looked just like a kid," Bergevin said.

But, post-game scrimmages aside, Marc-Andre didn't often act like a kid. His dad, Andre, and mom, France, would be proud to know their son required almost nothing in the way of guidance from his grizzled veteran of a roommate on how to carry himself properly on and off the ice.

"Even though he was young, he was mature," Bergevin said. "You hear stories about kids coming in with chips on their shoulders—that wasn't the case with Marc-Andre. He was very polite, (knew) his place and guys really enjoyed being around him 'cause he's such a good kid."

Marc-Andre's rise to the NHL ranks began in his hometown of Sorel, Que., just outside Montreal. Like many young French Canadians, he idolized butterfly goalie pioneer Patrick Roy and the ever-steady Martin Brodeur. But it was more than just the lure of being like his hockey heroes that pulled him into the crease. Something about being a fish on frozen water appealed to Marc-Andre. Not to mention the equipment is just plain cool.

"I just loved all the gear and flopping on the ice," said Marc-Andre of his early youth-hockey days in Sorel, where he would always beg his coaches to give him a chance to play goal. "I don't remember if I was good, but I just liked it."

Growing up in the goalie factory that was the province of Quebec in the 1990s, Marc-Andre had no shortage of competition for crease time. For proof of that consider the fact Marc-Andre, who in 2003 became just the third goalie in NHL history to be drafted first overall, didn't even get to start the final game when his Longueuil double-A team won the famous Quebec City peewee tournament.

"I played in the tournament, but not in the final," he recalled. "It was always tough to make the better teams. There was lots of competition."

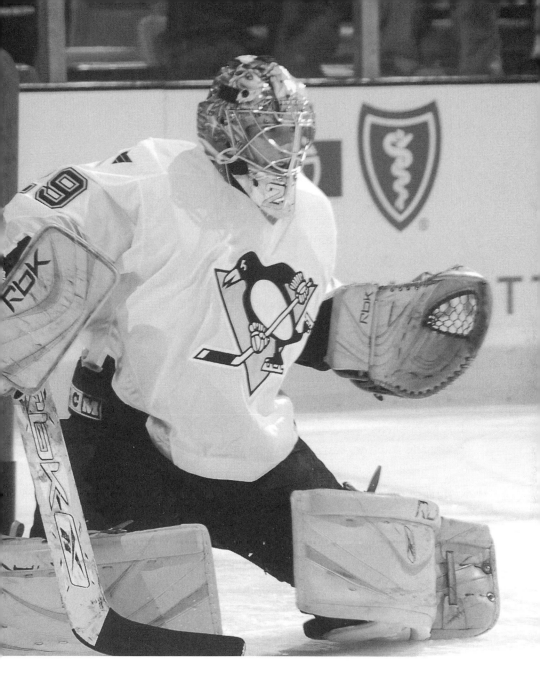

According to the goalie, stiffer standards just meant he had to raise the level of his play from a young age. But that doesn't mean he was immune to embarrassing plays. Even goalies with immense skill can sometimes be fooled by a funny bounce off the glass.

"I had a goal scored on me from the other zone, in peewee I think" Marc-Andre said. "The guy shot it from down at the other end, it hit the glass and it just bounced by me and they scored."

Shaking off incidents like that is much easier for people like Marc-Andre, who has incredible resolve and self-confidence. During his first year of major junior with the Quebec League's Cape Breton Screaming Eagles, Marc-Andre was pulled from a game after giving up a couple of soft goals. Eagles coach Pascal Vincent wanted his young stopper to have a project while he sat on the bench, so he handed him a clipboard and asked him to chart dangerous shots for both teams. After the final buzzer, the coach asked the kid for his homework. The front of the page was blank.

"After the game I saw that he didn't do anything so I was looking and there was a note on the back saying, 'I'm not a statistician, I'm a goaltender,' " Vincent explained.

Not surprisingly, the coach's first reaction was not a positive one. After all, a 16-year-old player had just flatly ignored his request.

"I was not too happy to see that, but on the other hand I could see he's got a lot of character," said Vincent, noting the Eagles didn't even think Marc-Andre would crack the roster that year until he blew them away at training camp. "So of course he was brought into the office and we had a few words—well he listened to the few words I had to say—but when he left we looked at each other, the coaching staff, and I remember saying, 'This kid is for real. He wants to play, maybe he made a mistake there, but he wants to play.' "

Marc-Andre's skill and character have both been tested at the annual World Junior Championship. In 2003, he put on a spectacular performance for Team Canada, claiming tournament MVP honours while carrying his team to the silver medal. The next year, Canada again advanced to the final only to lose to Team USA after an ill-advised clearing attempt by Marc-Andre hit teammate Braydon Coburn and went in the Canadian net for the decisive goal. Still, the fiery goalie persevered and, during Pittsburgh's resurgent 2006–07 season, Marc-Andre joined Tom Barrasso as the only Pens goalies to record 40-win seasons.

Throughout the highs and lows, Marc-Andre has kept his sense of humour. As much as fans and teammates admire him for his lightning-fast reflexes, Marc-Andre's light-hearted approach to things off the ice makes him a fun guy to be around. But as his roommate found out during one Pens road trip, if you let your guard down for too long around a genuine prankster, the results can be electric.

"One night in Florida, I'll never forget this, he came in from a store and he put a book next to my bed stand," Bergevin recalled. "It was like a joke book—I can't remember what the book was—but he just left it there and I grabbed the book and I started to open the page and it shocked me. He started laughing. He said he bought it at the bookstore and sure enough I grabbed it and he said 'I got you.'"

A noted prankster himself, Bergevin was not about to let the rookie off the hook so easily.

"It was my 20th year in the league and it was his first and he got me," he laughed. "About and hour later I said, 'Isn't it amazing, those books, if you grab them with your feet they won't shock you, it's just your hands.' He said, 'Really?' I said, 'Yes.' So he grabbed it with his toes and I got him."

Nobody said freshman goalies, no matter how good, aren't a little gullible.

★★ TIP   *"Being a good player takes focus and hard work, but more than anything the game should be fun. Make sure you're enjoying yourself on the ice."*

– RD

Ryan
Getzlaf

Always a Bruiser

Born:	May 10, 1985 – Regina, Sask.
First Team:	Sabres (Queen City Hockey)
Heroes:	Didn't have any
NHL Debut:	Oct. 5, 2005 at Chicago

I f anything was going to get Ryan Getzlaf's name in the newspaper headlines as a Western League rookie with the Calgary Hitmen, the smart money would have been on his deadly shot or propensity for slamming opponents into the boards. Instead, it was a slight oversight and ensuing tumble that landed Ryan a little attention he probably could have done without.

"The first year I went to Calgary, when I was 16, it was right after training camp and we had all the (hockey equipment representatives) come in for the first time and I had never really known what that was like," said the Anaheim Ducks centre.

Ryan, unfamiliar with the process of trying new equipment served up from the various companies, was anxious to break in a new pair of blades.

"I was trying on a pair of skates and the guy said I could try them out and I thought he meant right now," Ryan said.

After tightening the laces, the anxious rookie marched toward the ice to take a twirl with his new hockey footwear.

"I went out on the ice and the skates didn't actually have any steel in them," Ryan laughed.

As the freshman quickly found out, it doesn't matter how quality the plastic is, when it hits the ice in place of a skate blade, the person wearing the skates quickly follows suit.

As if a season's worth of teasing from teammates wouldn't be punishment enough, Ryan's gaffe actually made the local newspapers the next day. Not exactly a flying start to his major junior career.

However, most things went pretty smooth for Ryan when it came to playing hockey in his native Regina, Saskatchewan. He began skating when he was three and had a constant benchmark to measure up to in the form of his older brother, Chris.

"I started playing with my older brother," Ryan said. "Obviously we played on a lot of outdoor rinks back home when it was cold in the winter. I was always in competition with him growing up because I always wanted to be as good as he was. He was two years older than me, so he had a bit of a step on me."

Not that many players had a step on Ryan when he began playing novice hockey, coached by his dad, Steve.

Initially, Ryan was a defenceman who loved to make rink-long dashes with the puck. Noticing his son had great instincts on offence, Steve decided a position switch might be in order.

"I converted him," Steve laughed. "He started as a 'D' man and in his last year of novice I switched him from defence to forward. He was kind of a rushing defenceman and he was a really good playmaker. I think we had a few more 'D' that year than normal, so I moved him up to give him a shot at playing forward. He played centre and it worked out pretty good."

Ryan always had superb hand-eye coordination, which was part of the reason he was also an excellent baseball player. But even in the summer, when the bats got put away, the hockey sticks quickly came out.

"He learned a lot about stickhandling by playing shinny," Steve said. "They'd go play baseball and come home and play shinny."

Ryan said he never really rooted for one NHL team or player in particular growing up. He just loved to play the game.

The high point of Ryan's career was winning the Stanley Cup with the Ducks in just his second season in the NHL. But one of the early highlights came when he was chosen to play on a select summer team at the Vancouver Super Series novice tournament.

"At the time it was one of the biggest summer tournaments in the country," Steve said. "There were teams from all over the place."

The first year he went, Ryan was minor-novice age playing on a major-novice team comprised of players one year older than he was. That didn't stop him from being named to the tournament all-star team as the Regina squad took top spot at the event.

The next summer, playing with players his own age and coached by his father, Ryan was named tournament MVP as his team again advanced to the final, but this time it lost out in the championship game.

While he had excellent speed and skating abilities, there were other parts to Ryan's game that set him apart. If he wasn't blowing wide past a defender, he was trying to stuff a shot in the top shelf with his incredible wrist shot.

"When he was in novice he could shoot the puck from the blueline and put it under the crossbar," Steve said. "He scored a lot of goals like that."

Ryan, chosen 19th overall by the Ducks in 2003, constantly worked on firing the puck as a youth and still puts a heavy emphasis on honing that particular aspect of his game. It's not just about how hard—or even how accurate—the shot is, but how quickly the rubber gets off the tape.

"Your shot can get you a lot in this league and I always worked a lot on my shot when I was younger, and getting quicker releases," he said. "It's all about the quick release now and how fast you get that puck off when you're in stride."

At 6-foot-4 and 210 pounds, Ryan has made punishing, physical play a big part of his game, too. According to Steve, Ryan was a naturally aggressive player and was getting his nose dirty long before his body started shooting up and filling out.

"He took a few penalties along the line," Steve said. "He always liked the physical part of the game."

Hockey wasn't the only sport suited to Ryan's bruising nature. Both Getzlaf boys also played organized football growing up. "I actually loved football," Ryan said. "I played it for five or six years."

One year, when Ryan was roughly 12 years old, he and Chris formed a gridiron brother act that resulted in a slew of touchdown celebrations. Ryan formed the ground attack, pounding through opposing defences, while Chris provided the air strikes.

"Ryan was kind of a running back and Chris was a receiver and one year they scored 34 touchdowns between the two of them," Steve said. "It was pretty awesome."

Chris continues to pursue a career in football. After playing with the University of Regina Rams, he was drafted by the Hamilton Tiger-Cats in the Canadian Football League draft in May, 2007.

But, as evidenced by one telling flashpoint his father recalls, hockey was always more Ryan's game.

"He got chop-blocked when he was 12," Steve said. "I had to drive out on the football field and pick him up because he couldn't even walk."

Before Steve even had time to lift his injured son into the truck and cart him off to the hospital, Ryan, still draped in his football gear and lying on the field, expressed his biggest concern about being hurt.

"His exact words to me were, 'Dad, what about hockey?'" Steve relayed. "I said, 'We'll deal with this one day at a time.'"

Clearly Ryan, who spent a week on crutches after the injury, knew where his heart was.

"I loved (football), but hockey was a little bit more of a passion for me I guess," he said.

"Having a big shot helps you make an impression in this league. Shoot lots of pucks in practice and in the laneway so when you get a chance on the ice, you know you can bury it."

– RD

Phil
Kessel

Full Speed Ahead

Born: Oct. 2, 1987 – Madison, Wisc.

First Team: Southwest Eagles

Heroes: Any of the great players

NHL Debut: Oct. 6, 2006 at Florida

Ask Phil Kessel and he'll tell you Bob Suter was always there for him and is a big reason he's in the NHL today. Ask Bob about Phil and he'll tell you Phil was the reason the Madison Capitols believed they could win just about any game, even if they were trailing.

"They always knew Phil was there and he would always come through to get a goal or two to get us back in it or to win the game, or set somebody else up to do it," said Suter, who coached Phil from the time he was about seven years old up through his early teenage years. "You kind of always had confidence in him and what he could do.

"He had great speed even when he was young compared to a lot of other kids and he was just a natural goal-scorer."

Suter, who watched Phil tally 176 goals in one season as a 14-year-old bantam player, certainly knows the look of a star when he sees one. His younger brother, Gary Suter, had a stellar 17-year NHL career and Bob's son, Ryan Suter, is a young defenceman with the Nashville Predators. Bob also carved out his own piece of hockey history as a member of the 1980 Team USA 'Miracle on Ice' team which struck gold at the Olympics.

Reflecting back on his youth-hockey days in his hometown of Madison, Wisc., Phil had high praise for the coach who helped him so much on the path to becoming the fifth overall pick in the 2006 NHL draft.

"He was a real big influence on me," said Phil of Suter. "He helped me a lot in my career. He was my coach forever and he helped me become the player I am today."

Phil's dad, Phil Sr., believes Suter had a positive impact on his son's personality as well. No matter how much talent a player had, he always tried to make sure his head still fit inside his helmet.

"The best thing about Bob is he would never talk you up or anything like that," Phil Sr. said. "He made you work harder, I think, because he never said, 'You're a star.' He was the kind of guy who said, 'Work hard and in the end it will work out.' "

Phil's most memorable ride as a youth-hockey player came when his Capitols advanced all the way to the triple-A bantam national title game in Colorado Springs. The talented squad expected success, but couldn't quite overcome the bantam version of the L.A. Kings in the big game.

"We had a pretty good team that year, we didn't lose that many games and we went there, did pretty well—we just didn't win it," Phil said. "That was a tough one."

Like the Suters, the Kessels are an athletic bunch. Phil's dad was a star quarterback at Northern Michigan University and played with the Canadian Football League's Calgary Stampeders. Phil's mom, Kathy, was a high school track-and-field sprinter.

Phil's siblings, much like him, are more inclined toward the ice. Phil's younger brother, Blake, is a defenceman and was selected by the New York Islanders at the 2007 NHL draft while his younger sister, Amanda, won the 2007 under-19 national girls championship as a freshman with the famed high school hockey program at Shattuck St.-Mary's in Faribault, Minn.

Not surprisingly, family outings often involved athletics. Even when none of the kids was scheduled to be at the arena, the Kessels often found their way to the rink.

"We did a lot of packing them up on a Wednesday night when nobody had practice and we'd go to the outdoor rink or wherever there was skating," Phil Sr. said.

Despite his gridiron background, Phil Sr. never pushed the pigskin on his son.

"(Organized) football doesn't start until they're more in like fourth or fifth grade and then they're doing other stuff like hockey and we did a lot of soccer," Phil Sr. said. "In kindergarten and first grade, you're doing a lot of that stuff and when you have success with it, it's hard to get them to stop doing those things and go do the other stuff.

"It's a hard road, football. You have to be an awfully big guy to be a football player in most cases. The hockey seemed to suit (Phil) a little better."

And he was suited to hockey. Big time. The same October he turned 16, Phil left Madison for Ann Arbor, Mich. to play with the U.S. national team development program. In his two seasons there, Phil established new program records for career goals (104) and points (180). He also led Team USA to gold at the 2005 World under-18 Championship with an astonishing nine goals and 16 points in six games.

Phil Sr., always careful not to expect too much out of his son, said it took a while before he began to realize Phil was definitely a top-tier prospect.

"It wasn't early on because I'm a very conservative person so it wasn't like you're thinking, 'This kid is going to be some hot-shot player', " Phil Sr. said. "The first time we thought he might go on and do something was when he got picked for the developmental program in Ann Arbor. That was an early goal of his, to make that team."

But, in the mind of Phil Sr., success wasn't assured just because his son had cracked the squad.

"Then he made the team and there's a little apprehension when you got there because it's a whole bunch of guys who've been the best players on their team and you're not quite sure once you get there how it's going to work out," he said. "When other guys (from that program) started getting drafted like (Jack) Skille and (Jack) Johnson, it started to sink in."

Phil went on to win Western Collegiate Hockey Association rookie-of-the-year honours while suiting up for the University of Minnesota, before cracking the Bruins' lineup the following season. But reaching the NHL at the age of 19 wasn't the biggest challenge Phil faced in his first year. Not by a long shot.

Just months into his big-league career, Phil was diagnosed with testicular cancer.

"I never thought about dying," said Phil to *The Hockey News* at the time. "It does go through your mind, a little bit, but it wasn't the biggest thing. I didn't dwell on that. You have to stay positive, even though it's hard. You have to try. If you're miserable all the time and down, it's not going to do you any good."

Phil underwent successful surgery in Dec. 2006 and returned to the Boston lineup less than one month later. He went on to record a respectable 11 goals and 29 points in a 70-game rookie campaign, proving the kid who always had talent to burn had ample amounts of courage, too.

"I think he handled things extremely well," said Phil Sr. at the time. "The uncertainty of it was hard for him to handle and like anybody else, he was upset. But I was impressed with the strength he showed."

✦ ✦ TIP   *"Just have fun with the game. Always enjoy what you're doing on the ice."*

— RD

Anze
Kopitar

Slovenian Royalty

Born:	Aug. 24, 1987 – Jesenice, Slovenia
First Team:	Jesenice
Heroes:	Sergei Fedorov, Peter Forsberg
NHL Debut:	Oct. 6, 2006 at Anaheim

For Los Angeles Kings centre Anze Kopitar, it can seem the weight of an entire country's hockey aspirations is balanced on his shoulders. The small European nation of Slovenia boasts a population of just two million people, but one of those citizens happens to be among the most dynamic young stars in the NHL today.

"He has quite a high profile in his country," said Dave Taylor, who was GM of the Kings when the team drafted Anze 11th overall in 2005. "He has a certain prominence. There are a lot of natural leadership qualities in him."

Although Slovenia has produced half a dozen prominent NBA basketball players, Anze is the first international hockey star. He has certainly done his part to put his country on the map.

At the 2007 World Championship in Moscow, Anze tallied 14 points in just five games as Slovenia was promoted to the top level of play for the 2008 tournament. At the previous World Championship, he had scored 11 points as a 19-year-old.

Anze grew up in a hockey family. His father, Matjaz, played for their home-town team, Jesenice. Since Slovenia is so small, Jesenice is actually part of the Austrian League. Matjaz would coach Anze several times, including at the World Championship. Anze started skating at age three and a half. Soon after, his father built him a rink in the backyard.

"It was a really small surface," Anze said. "But good enough at the time."

Hanging out at the rink with his dad, Anze knew exactly what he wanted to be when he grew up.

"That's why I started. I loved to watch hockey," he said. "When he came home and brought me my own stick it was the greatest day of my life. I went right outside to the backyard and skated until my mom kicked me off because it was time for bed."

Anze would himself suit up for Jesenice, paving the way for a minor hock-ey career that was astounding to say the least.

At age 15, while playing for Jesenice's under-18 team, Anze racked up 38 goals and 76 points in just 14 games—an average of 5.5 points per con-test. As much fun as you might think that would be, it wasn't much of a challenge for a player hoping to grow his game.

"It was me and one other guy, we basically did all the work," Anze recalled. "Sometimes it got boring—it wasn't fun anymore. That's when I started to think about going somewhere else. I played up with the senior team for a while."

Even with the senior team, Kranjska Gora, Anze netted four goals and eight points in 11 games. In between, he had played for Jesenice's junior team and scored at more than a point-per-game pace.

The next year, as a 16-year-old, Anze again destroyed the junior ranks (60 points in 25 games) before once again heading to the senior league where he would add 25 points in 21 games. At this point, something had to be done to get Anze playing against suitable competition. He was playing only two or three hard games a month, but needed that push on a nightly basis. That's when Anze made the decision to take his act to Sodertalje in the Swedish Elite League.

"Of course it was hard to leave my family," Anze said. "But I was so focused on hockey."

Coming from Slovenia, Anze naturally didn't speak any Swedish, so he and his teammates communicated through a language familiar to both: English. He didn't know anyone there except his European agent, but soon fell in love with the higher calibre of hockey. He even gained a new idol.

"I (had) really liked Sergei Fedorov. He was basically my guy," Anze said. "But when I got to Sweden, it was Peter Forsberg."

Anze played well in Sweden, both in the junior and senior ranks. But come draft day, many teams were wondering if a Slovenian had the chops to make the NHL.

"It's not a natural background for a hockey player," Taylor admitted. "But his father was a coach and he led the Swedish junior league in scoring, so that says something."

Despite that endorsement, Anze slipped to 11th in the draft, where he was picked up by Taylor and the Kings. Los Angeles was more than happy to take a chance.

"He was actually the third-rated player on our list (behind Sidney Crosby and Jack Johnson)," Taylor noted. "He has a lot of qualities like Joe Thornton. He can handle the puck, he's a big body, and he has vision on the ice. There are really no weaknesses in his game and it comes in a big package."

For a player who came to North America essentially NHL-ready, Anze rarely got to watch the pro league as a child.

"There were a couple of games a month on TV, but my parents wouldn't let me stay up," Anze remembered. "There was a nine-hour time difference."

In fact, the first time Anze saw a game live wasn't until he was 17 when his agents at Newport Sports Management brought him over from Sweden.

The game was a playoff tilt between the Toronto Maple Leafs and Philadelphia Flyers, the last Stanley Cup tournament before the lockout—and Anze caught a classic.

"It was the night of the big hit: Darcy Tucker on Sami Kapanen," Anze noted. "That's when I saw the rough side of the NHL."

Not that Anze hadn't seen the rough side of life before. As a child, he had lived through Slovenia's war of independence, when the nation separated from Yugoslavia in 1991.

The Ten-Day War was, obviously, a brief conflict, but nonetheless very important to the people of Slovenia. Anze's father went to the field to fight for his nation while the family took shelter.

"We had a summer house in the mountains, so we just went there," Anze recalled. With the nation born under its own flag, the country flourished.

"You can really see the difference now," Anze said. "Slovenia's not a rich country, but it's much better off than some of the other (Baltic states)."

And even though Anze has embraced Los Angeles just as the city has embraced him—fans have been spraypainting a stencil of his face around town—he is still a proud Slovenian.

"Slovenia is really small," he said. "But we've got coast, mountains—a little bit of the Alps—there's some nice lakes that have tourist towns around them."

There's one other factor that keeps Anze's heart back home: "My girlfriend's there, too."

Having already put up stellar numbers in his first NHL season, Anze wants to keep spreading the gospel of his homeland.

"It feels really good to be the first guy. I'm just trying to get Slovenia on the hockey map right now," he said. "Hopefully I open up some spots in the draft for other Slovenian players."

In the meantime, Anze will be the centerpiece in a Kings organization bursting with young elite talent, including Patrick O'Sullivan and defenceman Jack Johnson, two rising young American players.

 *"The shootout drill. I like that one the best."*

– RK

Guillaume
Latendresse

Paying
His Dues

Born:	May 24, 1987 – Ste-Catherine, Que.
First Team:	Ste-Catherine Eagles
Hero:	Mario Lemieux
NHL Debut:	Oct. 6, 2006 at Buffalo

Long before he became a star for the Montreal Canadiens, defying the odds by making the team as a rookie teenager, and long before he could envision fans at the Bell Centre chanting his name each time he touched the puck, Guillaume Latendresse was like every other hockey prodigy. There were early-morning practices. Or bus rides to dilapidated barns that served as arenas.

"I never thought I'd be a pro. I played for fun," said the left winger, who cracked the Canadiens' roster as a 19-year-old out of training camp—his second stab at making the team—bypassing his final season of junior eligibility with Drummondville of the Quebec League in the process. "I was a bit sloppy and lazy, and didn't put much effort into it."

Guillaume's epiphany occurred when he was 14, when he met Martin Russell, a midget triple-A coach at College Charles Lemoyne, southeast of Montreal. Russell saw something in Guillaume that other minor-league coaches did not, and was able to get the most out of the big, gangly teenager, simply by gently prodding him.

"He changed the way I saw my career, and made me think I had a chance to play in the big league," Guillaume remembered. "I had a good season, and that gave me confidence."

Guillaume always had been big for his age. Indeed, he would be asked for his birth certificate at most tournaments as proof he wasn't overage. But he possessed just enough talent to often be advanced to an upper division, competing with and against older players. For example, he went directly from peewee to midget, bypassing the bantam level. Seeing that reservoir of skills, some coaches would criticize Guillaume, sapping him of his will. But Russell was different. He gave Guillaume the opportunity to play with his older brother, Olivier, a future draft choice of the Phoenix Coyotes. And it was Russell who put the younger Guillaume on the power play.

"(Russell) worked hard with me. And he knew me," Guillaume said. "That helped me a lot."

He wasn't a one-man wrecking crew, nor did he rewrite the record books, but Guillaume succeeded during his first year of midget, scoring 23 goals and 48 points in 39 games. Russell helped to eradicate the doubts Guillaume carried.

"He believed in me and worked with me," Guillaume said. "He gave me a chance to get ice time and to develop."

Today, some five years later, Russell denied doing anything special. He said it was obvious Guillaume possessed talent. Russell merely took advantage of the player's size.

"We talked as a staff. We thought he could play at that level, and we thought he could play right away," Russell remembered. "We knew him and saw him; saw the talent of the kid. We knew he had a lack of work ethic, but we worked hard with him to give him that. When he was in peewee, he was so much better than anyone else, so he didn't work enough. We got him to rise to the challenge of playing midget. When you give him a challenge, he's the best.

"But I'm not the one responsible for getting him to the NHL. After midget, he played major junior, where he had good coaching. But everyone who worked with him should have known he had talent."

Guillaume started skating in his hometown of Ste-Catherine, Que., when he was three, and played for his first youth team two years later. He always was used at forward.

"I was good maybe because I was bigger, and that would put me ahead of the other kids," he remembered. "Skating was always an issue. It still is."

He remembers coaches—even at the peewee level—being tough on him, attempting to get more from the prodigious talent. Guillaume also remembers his parents supporting him and his brother through all endeavours. If the boys had tournaments in different cities, their mother, Linda, would be with one and their father, Alain, with the other. And no destination was deemed too far, even if that meant boarding an airplane for Minnesota or Boston. Resources were never an issue, either. Guillaume took power-skating lessons for three years once he reached the junior level.

"I was always laughing with my parents," Guillaume said. "My father used to tell me all of my skill (was inherited) from him. But my brother and me were lucky. Wherever we played, my parents, even my grandparents, were there. They would do whatever was necessary to make sure we played good hockey. We were lucky to have great people like that behind us."

Alain Guillaume said he never complained about driving to practices or games. He was happy to lend support or offer advice, when necessary, but emphasized never putting pressure on the future Canadien.

"I would go with Guillaume to the arena, and I don't stop now," he said. "I never corrected what he was doing, only trying to help him. I encouraged him to like hockey...to like playing. But I never put pressure on him. Never, never. He played for fun. It was only when he reached major junior that he needed to be serious."

Guillaume was on the ice morning and night while growing up. There was no such thing as too much hockey. Even when he was a midget, between practices and games, Guillaume rarely was away from the rink. His style of play was defined early, and he usually could be found around the net, waiting for rebounds.

Guillaume, by now one of the province's leading power forwards, went second overall—behind Sidney Crosby—to Drummondville in the 2003 Quebec League draft of graduating midgets. Although Guillaume made the QMJHL rookie all-star team, his statistics were ordinary, scoring 24 goals and 49 points in 53 games. He was better his second season, producing 29 goals and 49 assists in 65 games, leading the Canadiens to select him 45th overall in the 2005 entry draft.

But even that wasn't enough for Dominic Ricard, the Voltigeurs' coach and GM at the time.

"Sometimes, I was a bit lazy," Guillaume admitted. "Even if I had a good game, he (Ricard) wanted more and pushed me. Sometimes I was frustrated and wanted to fight him, but if I'm here (in the NHL) today, he's part of the reason why. At the time it wasn't fun. But now I can see he wanted to help me. He would criticize me in public. Then after, in private, tell me he was doing it for me."

Guillaume matured as a person during the 2005–06 season, when he was the Canadiens' final cut at training camp. It wasn't easy going from the front page of Montreal newspapers back to the relative anonymity of major junior, and he struggled upon his return to Drummondville. Although he made Canada's team for the World Junior Championship, Guillaume eventually was demoted, becoming the club's 13th forward.

"He was 24 hours away from being a millionaire," said Ricard at the time. "He came back here and we're giving him $50 a week."

Guillaume eventually found his niche, scoring 43 goals and 83 points in just 51 games for the Voltigeurs. He returned to Montreal's camp in September 2006 with more resolve. He was better prepared and wanted to prove things to management.

Guillaume had an up and down year in his rookie season. He went on a scoring tear in November, while playing on a line with Saku Koivu, but then endured a prolonged slump. Then, Guillaume scored five goals over a six-game span in March, and completed the season with 16 goals and 29 points in 80 games.

"Guillaume came up (in his rookie year) and a lot of people said it was because he's French," said Canadiens coach Guy Carbonneau. "But he deserved to be here. He's been a better player—not because of his offence, but because of his defence. I'm not afraid to use him in any situation."

★ ★ TIP
"It depends on your strength. If it's skating, practise your shot. Whenever you have time to play, practise your weakness."
– Herb Zurkowsky

Kari
Lehtonen

The Kid
from Helsinki

Born:	Nov. 16, 1983 – Helsinki, Finland
First Team:	TJV Helsinki
Hero:	Jarmo Myllys
NHL Debut:	March 19, 2004 vs. Florida

You would think being one of the NHL's youngest starting goaltenders would be an intimidating prospect, but Atlanta's Kari Lehtonen is used to being the youngest on the ice.

Kari, who grew up in Helsinki, Finland, first discovered his love of hockey by watching his older brother play.

"I would go to the rink and watch him," Kari said. "He told me how much fun it was, so I wanted to do it, too."

The next year Kari did just that, taking to the ice for local club TJV as a forward. But being just five years old, Kari was dwarfed in both size and skill by the other players.

"Everyone else was three years older," he recalled. "I felt that I didn't do very well because the other guys were so much bigger, but I loved the game, so I wanted to keep playing."

The next year, Kari donned the goalie pads. He hasn't looked back since.

As a child, Kari was fortunate to grow up in a neighbourhood filled with youngsters and spent a great deal of his free time playing sports.

"In the housing complex I lived in there were about 10 kids all around the same age," he said. "We would play all kinds of sports 24/7: soccer, baseball—that was great for me and it helped me be more athletic."

Of course, in the winter, there wasn't as much daylight to play in since Finland is just below the Arctic Circle. "The winters are extremely long," Kari said. "It's kind of like Alaska."

After several years with TJV, Kari was in need of better competition. Jokerit, which means 'the Jokers' in Finnish, is one of the country's biggest squads, but in Europe a player generally stays with the same team their whole youth.

"I think my mom called the coach to see if I could try out," he said, "and I was invited to practise with them."

Kari's skills were more than adequate and Jokerit became his new home club.

The coolest part about joining the squad was that all the young players got season tickets to see the Jokerit pro team, which played in Finland's top league, the SM-Liiga.

"That was awesome," Kari remembered. "We'd go to their practices, too. They were big, big, idols for me. I would watch them and think 'if I work hard I have a chance to make that team.' "

Those teams included a couple of future NHLers whom Kari would eventually follow to North America: Ossi Vaananen of the Colorado Avalanche and Jani Rita, who played for Edmonton and Pittsburgh before returning to Jokerit in 2006.

Ironically, Kari's idol at the time didn't even play for his home team; Kari liked Lukko Rauma goaltender Jarmo Myllys, who is a hero in Finland for his international play. He is a former NHLer who played with the Minnesota North Stars and San Jose.

But it was another veteran Finnish goaltender who would change Kari's life forever.

Jarmo 'Jammi' Kauppi was a goalie by trade, but by the time Kari met him, he was coach of Jokerit's Jr. A team.

"I was pretty good at 15 years old, playing for the Jr. C team," Kari recalled. "He would come to our practices and said he thought if I worked hard I could become very good."

Kauppi, who now coaches Jokipojat in Finland's second division, remembers how he saw greatness early in Kari, especially because of his size (today, Kari's 6-foot-4).

"He was so tall," Kauppi said. "He reminded me of an old-style goalie, like Ken Dryden."

Kauppi invited Kari to join the Jr. A team during the summer, so the young-ster could train and practise with the team. Once again, Kari was the baby of the bunch; most of the other players were 20 or 21 years old, while he was still just 16.

Then, on the eve of the new season, Jokerit's starting Jr. A goaltender wrecked his knee. Kauppi turned to his teenage phenom to fill the void.

"In the first game, he played so well," Kauppi recalled. "Next game, same style."

With the confidence of having his coach behind him, Kari kept playing well for the whole season and Jokerit went all the way, winning the champi-onship. Kari notched four shutouts in 12 playoff games and posted an out-standing 1.11 goals-against average.

"Now that I think back about it, maybe that was the biggest step in my career," Kari said. "We were on the ice together every day doing drills. I owe a lot to him."

Kari would spend the next couple of years bouncing between the junior team and the men's team, where, playing against some guys old enough to be his father, he never let his goals-against average rise above 1.90.

In 2002, the Atlanta Thrashers drafted Kari in the first round, second over-all behind Columbus' Rick Nash. After another year with Jokerit, he was assigned to Atlanta's farm team in the American League, the Chicago Wolves. The adjustment was difficult and Kari learned an important lesson.

"I didn't do great in school—hockey was on my mind too much—so when I came over here, I couldn't speak English," he said. "That first year, I didn't speak basically at all."

It was also his first year living on his own, as he had always lived with his family before then.

There was some good news at the end of the season, however. With the playoffs out of reach, the Thrashers wanted to test their new draft pick out. Kari was called up to the NHL, where he won all four games in which he played, giving up just five goals for a GAA of 1.25.

After spending the lockout season back with the Wolves in Chicago, Kari was expected to help the Thrashers reach their first-ever playoff berth in 2005–06, but things did not go as planned. Coach Bob Hartley openly criticized Kari's conditioning when he came to training camp and in the first game of the season, the young goalie injured his groin. Kari missed more than half of the season due to various injuries and the Thrashers missed the playoffs. Again, Kari learned a valuable lesson.

"The biggest part of a goalie's work is to be mentally tough," he said. "(That) year I was worrying too much about bad games; good games I was way too happy. Now, when a game is over, I try not to think about it too much. The next game is the only one you can have an effect on."

Kari said he gets a boost when his family, who lives in Finland, visits him in North America. His brother usually comes over with a friend, his sister comes with her family and his parents come together once a season. Along with getting to spend time with them (Kari would like to see them more often), he also gets to eat his mom's home cooking, something he misses dearly. What's his favourite dish?

"It's this weird meat sauce with mashed potatoes," he said. "That's the one thing I always ask for when I go home in the summer."

✦ ✦ TIP   *"Goalies should get on the ice a half-hour before the rest of the guys at practice. You have to be well warmed up when they come on the ice—otherwise when you start, you can get injured."*
— RK

Andrej
Meszaros

The 'All-Canadian' Slovak

Born:	Oct. 13, 1985 – Povazska Bystrica, Slovakia
First Team:	Povazska Bystrica
Hero:	Pavel Bure
NHL Debut:	Oct. 5, 2005 at Toronto

When Andrej Meszaros is patrolling the blueline for the Ottawa Senators, he does so with the poise of a crafty veteran, even though the defenceman has actually been on the NHL stage for only two seasons. He's just that good.

"He's very mature—he has an 'old soul' I heard someone say once," said defence partner Wade Redden, a veteran of 10 NHL seasons. "And he's a strong man for his age."

Perhaps that's because Meszaros was a quick study and willing student under fellow Slovakian defenceman and Bruins behemoth Zdeno Chara, his partner as a rookie in Ottawa.

"He taught me to go into the corners, look behind my shoulder and move as fast as I can," Andrej said. "It was up to me how I did."

When it comes to motivation, Andrej has always had the fire. Growing up in Slovakia as that nation was splitting with the Czech Republic (it had been one country named Czechoslovakia before 1993), Andrej started playing hockey at age six for his hometown team, Povazska Bystrica. The town has a rich history, with references to it dating back to the year 1330, but it is still a quiet place.

"It's a small city," Andrej said. "Now there are about 60,000 people living there, but when I left it was only 45,000."

When Andrej's skills as a youth began to shine, it was time for him to move up in the Slovakian hockey world. At age 12, he left Povazska Bystrica to play for Dukla Trencin, a powerhouse team that has produced NHL stars such as Minnesota's Pavol Demitra and Marian Gaborik, as well as Chara.

"My team was in a small league, so I went to Trencin, which is in the big league," Andrej said.

It was there where Andrej would hone the skills and work ethic instilled in him by his father, Lubos Meszaros, who had also played for Povazska Bystrica and coached Andrej as a youth.

"He was tough on me," Andrej noted. "I couldn't do anything easy, I couldn't cheat, I had to do it right. He wanted me to be the best on the ice. I'd even stay after practice sometimes and do extra skating."

It was that extra training that put Andrej in such a good position among young players in his country and prepared him for numerous international tournaments where he would make his mark on the world stage.

He served as captain on several Slovakian national junior teams, including the silver medal-winning under-18s in 2003 and the 2005 world junior squad. Andrej also made his mark early, as the youngest member of both the 2004 Slovakian junior team and national team that played at the World Championship that same year.

It was that senior team that would expose Andrej to one of the most impressive lineups of Slovak talent ever. The roster included NHLers Gaborik, Demitra, Marian Hossa, Miroslav Satan, Jozef Stumpel and, of course, Chara.

"It was something I'll never forget," Andrej said. "It was unbelievable."

The young defenceman with the will to learn hadn't even been drafted yet and he was holding his own amongst the best players in the world, recording an even plus-minus in seven games.

That summer, Andrej was the first selection taken by the Senators, but instead of staying in Europe or going to the American League, he opted for a year of Canadian major junior hockey, suiting up for the Vancouver Giants.

"It is North American-style hockey," Andrej noted. "Even if I stayed in the men's league in Europe, I think junior gave me the right experience. It's physical, I like that style. It worked out well."

Andrej excelled on the ice with the Giants, recording 11 goals and 41 points in 59 games, but he also made a big impression off the ice, as well.

"He struck me as a well-put-together young man," said Elaine Larmour, billet co-coordinator for the Giants and the woman who took Andrej in. "He almost fit in right away—he seemed to be very North American."

And it's a good thing Andrej and the Larmour family got along; the first time they met was the first night Andrej was to stay with them.

"We had no idea what he was like," Larmour said. Vancouver officials brought Andrej straight from the plane to a restaurant called White Spot, where he would meet Elaine for the first time and introduce himself.

Larmour had taken a special interest in European players and told the team to send one her way. Since major junior teams can only have two Europeans on the roster, it is often a difficult transition for them—even if the other import speaks your native language, that's still only one person to talk to.

Nevertheless, Larmour, who also billeted Czech goalie and St. Louis Blues prospect Marek Schwarz, has very fond memories of Andrej's time in Vancouver.

"He was an addition to our family," she said. According to Larmour, when he wasn't on the ice, Andrej liked clothes shopping and spent a good deal of time renting movies. "He was quite the homebody."

After just one season with the Giants, Andrej made the jump to the NHL, where he would be aligned once again with his mentor, Zdeno Chara. The two played much of the season as defensive partners, with Andrej racking up an impressive plus-34, putting him among the best in the entire league, let alone among rookies.

"It was like a big brother kind of relationship," Redden observed. " 'Z' took him under his wing, for sure. The way he works, the way he competes— plus, with speaking the same language, that was a real help."

But the mentorship would last just a single season. Chara was one of the most coveted free agents in the NHL and went to Boston. Andrej still cherishes their time together, short as it was.

"He told me what's going on here," Andrej said. "He was there for me on the ice and off the ice. It was sad to see him go to Boston, but that's hockey."

In his second season, Andrej continued to log major minutes, this time with Redden as his partner.

And while the North American-style defenceman loves Ottawa, he still pines for his home back in Povazska Bystrica every once and awhile.

"I miss the mountains," Andrej said. "We had really nice mountains. In Ottawa you can drive an hour or so to Mont Tremblant, but there aren't any in the city."

Well, unless you count the 6-foot-2, 215-pound one manning the blueline.

"(Practising) 1-on-1 is the best for forwards and defencemen, especially in the new NHL where so much of it comes down to 1-on-1s. You can challenge yourself with them."

– RK

Rick Nash

Hockey by the Headlights

Born:	June 16, 1984 – Brampton, Ont.
First Team:	Brampton Maroons
Heroes:	Doug Gilmour, Mats Sundin
NHL Debut:	Oct. 10, 2002 vs. Chicago

Supporting a young hockey player usually means frequent trips to the sporting goods store for sticks, skates and other equipment necessities. In the case of Jamie Nash, it also meant scooping up the occasional car battery to make sure his son, Rick Nash, could get in all the skating he wanted during his initial spins on the ice.

Growing up in the Toronto suburb of Brampton, Ont., Rick began skating on a pond nestled inside the confines of his neighbourhood. Darkness usually dictates when outdoor games end, but in the case of Rick and his older brother, James, it was an intrusion they didn't have to succumb to thanks to their dad.

"We'd go (to the pond) at night after dinner and he'd turn the car on and put the lights on and we'd just skate and play as long as we could," Rick said.

When the games inevitably did come to an end, it didn't necessarily mean Rick was done with hockey for the night. Often he just switched venues from the pond to the living room, where he'd plunk down in front of the TV to watch his favourite team.

"I was a huge Leafs fan," said the left winger, who was drafted first overall by the Columbus Blue Jackets in 2002. "(Doug) Gilmour and (Mats) Sundin were kind of my two guys that I always watched."

Nash began playing organized hockey with the Brampton Maroons, though some of his fondest memories are from times when his team was playing far away from his hometown. "The biggest thing was always just going to travel tournaments, like to Buffalo, when you're so young, staying in hotels and playing mini-sticks in the halls and hide-and-seek in the hotels with security guards chasing you," Rick laughed.

Though he didn't know it at the time, his early trips to hotels served as a small sampling of what his life in the NHL would eventually be like. "I used to love staying in hotels and now, at this level, your whole life is in hotels so it's funny how it comes full circle," Rick said.

Hockey wasn't the only outlet for Rick's natural sporting ability. He was also a talented lacrosse player and played the sport every summer up until the age of 15. There's no doubt in Rick's mind playing lacrosse helped develop the quick hands which allowed him to tie Calgary's Jarome Iginla and Atlanta's Ilya Kovalchuk for the NHL goal-scoring title during the 2003–04 season, just his second in the league.

"I think it was great, especially for the hands," said Rick of lacrosse. "There's lots of NHLers who play lacrosse like (Brendan Shanahan and Joe Nieuwendyk). I think it really helps with the hands."

But Rick's soft hands didn't save him from every hard situation on the ice. Take, for instance, one game he played as an eight-year-old when he had a very difficult time keeping both feet moving in the same direction. The problem was rooted in a trip to the rink he took with friends and family the night before.

"We all went public skating the night before and everyone threw their skates in the trunk," Rick said. "So the next day I had a game and I just opened the trunk and grabbed the skates, and my buddy had the same pair, so I ended up playing the game with two right skates on."

Equipment mix-ups aside, Rick faced one of his first big challenges in hockey when he opted to make the move as a 10-year-old to play up the road in the big city.

"I don't know how it is now, but back then they always said the best players were in Toronto," recalled Rick, who joined the Toronto Marlboros' triple-A club as an atom player. "I think that was kind of intimidating for me, going from my hometown and regular hockey to the (Toronto) league."

Rick's move to Toronto fortuitously coincided with another shift. Keith Carrigan, a man who had exclusively coached older teenage hockey players, was asked if he would guide the Marlboros' atom entry. Carrigan wasn't sure how he'd take to the young kids at first, but decided to give it a try. That decision forged a teacher-student relationship with Rick that continues to this day when the two get together each summer to work on skills to improve Rick's game.

"Rick was glued to everything I said," Carrigan recalled. "When you're in a dressing room and you're talking to kids, most kids have an attention span of about 10 seconds. Rick had a very long attention span when it came to hockey. When I would talk he would stop whatever he was doing right away. He would look at me—and one thing about Rick to this day—when I'm talking to him he's staring at me and it's like he's staring right through me. He really gets focused on every word I'm saying." And what Carrigan was teaching Rick—and the rest of the young Marlboros—was far from kids' stuff.

"The major thing about him is we started doing drills (in atom) that I'm doing now in the NHL," Rick said. "It just seemed he was so advanced to be coaching at that level."

With the exception of one year, Carrigan coached Rick right up until the time he moved from Toronto to play major junior with the Ontario League's London Knights. While Rick eventually blossomed into a 6-foot-4, 215-pound man, what caught Carrigan's attention about Rick from Day 1 is how strong he was between the ears.

"Rick challenged himself in everything we ever did to be the best," Carrigan said. "Everything I'd be teaching, it could just be a simple drill, he wanted to be the best at it. And he would work very, very hard to be the absolute best at every one of those aspects of the game."

His MVP performance at the 2007 World Championship proved that the big Blue Jacket is clearly capable of elevating his game in big moments. Carrigan said Rick has always made a habit of gritting his teeth and finding a way to get the job done when the game is on the line. Take, for example, his performance in a do-or-die shootout as a 13-year-old in the famous Quebec City peewee tournament. As the Marlboros' final shooter, Rick had a chance to send his team through to the next round if he could find a way to solve a stopper from Alberta that was giving his teammates fits.

"Rick came to me and asked, 'What do you think coach?', " Carrigan relayed. "I said, 'Rick, I think you've got to fake one way and then go between his legs.' Now you can imagine, this is a peewee kid, a 13-year-old kid, and I've just told him to fake one way, pull the goalie over and there's going to be this little hole between his legs and you've got to put the puck there. He looked at me and said, 'OK, coach', and off he went and I think there were about 12,000 people in the rink or something and he goes out and executes that play.

"I thought afterwards, that was way too much pressure to put on a 13-year-old kid. But you know what, it didn't phase him."

"Practice makes perfect. Work on your skills, hone them, pay attention to detail and you'll surely see results in your game."

– RD

Rostislav
Olesz

Olympic Dreams

Born:	Oct. 10, 1985 – Bilovec, Czech Republic
First Team:	Vitkovice
Heroes:	Jaromir Jagr, Vaclav Varada
NHL Debut:	Oct. 5, 2005 vs. Atlanta

Rostislav Olesz is a big fan of the European school of hockey training.

Growing up in the Czech Republic, Rostislav played for the Vitkovice team in the town of Ostrava, where he grew up. Rostislav, born in nearby Bilovec, moved to the nation's third-largest city as a child and stuck with the Vitkovice Steel program for nearly his entire youth career before coming to Florida in 2005–06. That steadiness was a positive for the emerging talent.

"It's very good, I like it," Rostislav said. "You play with the same guys every year for maybe nine years." Along with seeing players at the rinks, Rostislav also saw some future prospects in other places around town.

"I sat at the same table at school with (defenceman) Roman Polak from the St. Louis Blues," he added.

Along with hockey, Rostislav also spent time as a child playing sports such as tennis, handball and soccer. "Over there it's hockey in the winter and soccer in the summer," he said.

Rostislav said he didn't play hockey in the streets as a child; he and his buddies found other places to play. "We played behind the house, or at the playground—10, 15 guys," he noted. "It was a small challenge."

Rostislav started playing hockey at age four, in the same year that his older brother started. Going through the Vitkovice system, the team would sometimes travel for games—Rostislav remembers wearing his skates on the bus—but Vitkovice's home rink hosted several teams, so often it played in the same place. And it wasn't exactly the best rink.

"Ask Rostislav about that," laughed Washington Capitals left winger Tomas Fleischmann, who also played for Vitkovice. "Where we started, it was like a practice rink for peewees."

And while Rostislav has fond memories of the old barn, he also points out that things are changing in his home country.

"Now it's very good," he noted. "When we won the championship in Prague (when Rostislav played for Sparta Praha), they built a new arena. The arenas don't hold 17,000, they hold more like 7,000 to 8,000, but they are nice. Everything's about money. Sometimes it happens, sometimes it doesn't."

The state of those local rinks was historically controlled by the Soviet Union, which ruled over what was then known as Czechoslovakia until a revolution in 1989. Four years later, the country split in two, becoming the independent states of Slovakia and the Czech Republic.

"When the Czech Republic was part of Russia, nothing got done," Rostislav noted. "It's much better now."

Along with improvements in the quality of life, the fledgling nation also sought out a hockey identity; two new countries meant the powerhouse Czechoslovakian team was now split as well and both wanted to show off on the world stage.

The Czech Republic won that opportunity first, thanks to the 1998 Winter Olympics in Nagano, Japan, the first to feature NHL players. While Canada was heavily favored in the tournament, the Czech team rode the play of stars Jaromir Jagr and Dominik Hasek all the way to the gold medal. Meeting Team Canada in the semifinal, the Czechs pushed the game to a shootout. Robert Reichel scored on the first attempt for the Czechs and Hasek stopped all five Canadian shooters for the victory. Controversially, Wayne Gretzky did not participate in the shootout.

After dispatching with the Canadians, the underdogs took on their nemesis, Russia, for the gold. Once again, Hasek was superb as the Czechs won 1-0 on a third period goal by Petr Svoboda.

For Rostislav, who was 13 at the time, seeing those games was a life-changing experience, though a difficult one to coordinate at times. "Because of the time change in Nagano, sometimes I came to school late, or I would walk around the school looking for a TV," he recalled. "Everybody was so happy when we won."

Rostislav continued to follow the stars of that squad, even though getting NHL games in Ostrava wasn't easy. "Growing up, the only NHL player anyone knew was Jaromir Jagr," he said. "I liked Jagr, but my second-favourite player was Vaclav Varada, who plays in Switzerland now. He was a tough guy and he played for Vitkovice. I practise with him in the summer now."

Another player he sees in the summer is Fleischmann, who has known Rostislav since he was 10. The two played together in the Vitkovice system and used to have pretty good chemistry together when they were line-mates. "We had fun," Fleischmann said. "We had some set-up plays for faceoffs."

Nowadays the pair still sees each other in the winter, but it's on opposite sides of the Southeast Division rivalry between Rostislav's Panthers and Fleischmann's Capitals.

"We always see each other after the games when we shake hands," Fleischmann noted.

Rostislav played most of 2006–07 on Florida's top line with Jozef Stumpel and team captain Olli Jokinen. While Rostislav has never put up big offensive numbers in his career, his positioning is solid and as a sophomore, the Panthers trusted him with a good deal of penalty-killing responsibilities. Florida ended up with the 16th-best penalty-kill in the league, which isn't bad for a team that missed the playoffs in 2007.

Of course, taking on challenges at a young age is nothing new to Rostislav. While playing for Vitkovice in 2000–01, Rostislav became the youngest player ever to compete in the Czech Elite League, besting the previous record held by the legendary Jagr. The next season, he scored his first goal in the men's league at age 16. He played parts of five seasons in the Elite League even before he was an NHL rookie at age 20.

Rostislav came to Florida in 2005, playing 59 games in his rookie season for the Panthers and tallying eight goals and 21 points. That season, he also got to play for the same Czech Olympic team he idolized as a boy, a team that once again included Jagr and Hasek.

Of course, going straight from the Czech Republic to south Florida was an adjustment for the young man. "Europe is different from America," Rostislav said. "We don't have big downtowns."

Indeed, back in Ostrava, the main industries, historically, were coal mining and steelworks, which is why the hockey team is named the Vitkovice Steel. Work is a big part of the culture there.

"The life is different," Rostislav noted. "In America, everyone has time to do things (other than work)." He also misses his native land's natural features.

"Ostrava's 15 minutes from the mountains," he said. "Slovakia's nearby, Poland is nearby. It's nice."

Despite spending most of his year in a country far different from the one he grew up in, Fleischmann says Rostislav hasn't changed much since he was a kid.

"He's still the same guy," he said. "He's a real fun guy. It's really good to be around him."

With a bright future ahead of him, that's something his teammates in Florida already know.

✦ **DRILL**   *"I do a lot of shooting, especially in the summer. I take 25 pucks and fire them four times into each corner of the net as a warm-up."*

— RK

Alex
Ovechkin

A Dynamo from Day 1

Born:	Sept. 17, 1985 – Moscow, Russia
First Team:	Moscow Dynamo (youth team)
Hero:	Owen Nolan
NHL Debut:	Oct. 5, 2005 vs. Columbus

Given his lineage, Alex Ovechkin's ascent to NHL glory seems only natural. Yet in some ways, it's a small wonder the Russian star has accomplished all he has.

Alex definitely comes by his athletic genes honestly. His father, Mikhail, was a professional soccer player. His mother, Tatiana, was a very accomplished basketball player. She won two Olympic gold medals while competing for the former Soviet Union's national women's basketball squad in 1976 and 1980.

But just because they were able to pass on some serious athleticism to their son doesn't mean Tatiana and Mikhail always had time to take him to the rink. At one point as a youngster, Alex had to stop playing hockey for a number of months because there was simply no way to get him to practice and games all the time.

"Nobody had time to take me to practice, my mom and dad were busy," Alex said.

That's when his older brother, Sergei, stepped in for the second time in Alex's young career. He made sure his little brother had his equipment bag packed and a way to get to the arena so he could continue pursuing his dream of becoming a hockey player. In fact it was Sergei, when Alex was eight years old, who got the charismatic right winger playing hockey in the first place.

"My older brother took me to a hockey school and I just started playing," said Alex, who grew up in Moscow and has another older brother who shares the name Mikhail with his dad.

Tragically, when Alex was just 10, Sergei, in his early 20s, was killed in a car accident. Dealing with the loss of a loved one is a process that can only truly be understood by those who have been through it. With the person who got him into hockey and kept him in the game gone, it would have been easy to understand if Alex lost the motivation to play. But, according to brother Mikhail, that never crossed Alex's mind.

"It was a shock for all of us, but he didn't stop playing hockey," he said. "He kept going."

Unlike NHL teams, Russian Super League clubs have youth programs that reach down to the very roots of hockey. Because of that, Alex began playing in the Moscow Dynamo system from the very start of his hockey career.

Years before Alex began playing in the Russian Super League, he was already making a name for himself in the Dynamo system by breaking a goal-scoring record previously set by one of his most famous countrymen.

"I remember, when I was a kid I had 53 goals and Pavel Bure at the same age scored 56," recalled Alex, who was 11 at the time. "I scored six goals in our last game and I beat that record."

For many young players, half the fun of scoring goals is trying to emulate the moves they see their favourite players making on TV. Kids who grew up watching Denis Savard wanted to do the spin-o-rama. Everybody who admired Mario Lemieux always wanted to shoot top shelf. But that wasn't the case for Alex, who didn't really have much of a chance to see a lot of NHL action.

"It was hard to watch the NHL in Russia because I didn't have a special TV, but I read the newspaper and I knew about the NHL," Alex said.

A big part of his exposure came in the form of hockey cards and he remains an avid collector of hockey memorabilia to this day. Even though his NHL experience was mainly limited to still pictures, Alex had an affinity for Owen Nolan and the San Jose Sharks as a youngster.

His combination of goals and grit—maybe he was watching Nolan after all?—earned Alex lots of attention from high-ranking Russian hockey brass. At 16, Alex broke the World Under-18 Championship scoring record (previously held by fellow Russian Ilya Kovalchuk) with 14 goals and 18 points in eight games. He also won a World Junior Championship gold medal and, at 17, became the youngest player ever to suit up for the Russian men's national team, guided by legendary coach Victor Tikhonov. Eventually, Alex would follow in his mother's footsteps and participate in the Olympics, scoring six goals in seven games at the 2006 Winter Olympics in Turin, though his Russian crew finished out of the medals. Alex shared some advice his mother gave him on the Olympic experience with *The Hockey News* just after the tournament ended.

"She tell me it was great emotions and great experience, but she win and I not," he said. "It's OK, I have lots of time to win."

His early international exploits garnered Alex all kinds of attention in North America. Born Sept. 17, 1985, Alex missed the cut-off for the 2003 draft by a mere two days. For an indication of how sought after Alex was, consider the fact that the crafty Florida Panthers tried (likely knowingly in vain) to lobby the league that if leap years were taken into account, Alex would technically qualify for the '03 draft. By that flimsy logic, the Cats thought they had a better chance to get their claws into Alex. However, to nobody's surprise, the league didn't bite, and Alex wound up the crown jewel of the 2004 draft, going first overall to Washington.

On the heels of the lockout, Alex entered the league alongside Pittsburgh Penguins wunderkind Sidney Crosby, and the two seem destined for career-long comparisons as they each posses superb talents and battle head-to-head four times a season in the Eastern Conference. Alex won Round 1 with Sidney by taking the Calder Trophy as rookie of the year in 2005–06 as he popped 52 goals in an unforgettable freshman campaign.

But playing against men 15 years his senior and stingy NHL defensive schemes weren't the only challenges Alex faced in leaving his homeland behind. He had to learn a new language, new culture and face the crush of media attention his talent warrants.

"It was difficult for him, but he knew some (of the) language," said the 25-year-old Mikhail, who also made the voyage to Washington with his brother, as the two were roommates during Alex's first two years with the Caps.

As the hockey world quickly found out, 'Ovie' has just as much style off the ice as on it, flashing an infectious grin and enthusiasm for the game at every turn. Speaking the international language of 'he shoots, he scores!' helped bridge a lot of gaps, too. Alex had 98 goals through 163 games in two seasons. His most famous—and one of the league's best in recent memory—saw him sneak a puck past Phoenix goalie Curtis Joseph from a seemingly impossible angle while sliding on his back and facing the blue-line.

Anybody who has seen Alex celebrate after each tally can tell you the guy simply has a passion for putting the puck in the net. There's a reason for all the fist-pumping and glass-slamming he does. According to Mikhail, filling the net has always added up to fun for Alex.

"I remember (when he was young) his team was playing another team and they won like 25 to 6—that's an approximate score—and he scored that day probably 14 goals," Mikhail recalled. "It was probably the most fun day ever for him."

And there are plenty more ahead.

✦ ✦ TIP   *"The best thing you can do is to listen to your parents. You don't always see it, but they are always looking out for you and know what's best. I always trusted my mom and dad."*

– RD

Zach
Parise

The
Natural

Born:	July 28, 1984 – Minneapolis, Minn.
First Team:	Bloomington-Jefferson Jaguars
Hero:	Mike Modano
NHL Debut:	Oct. 5, 2005 vs. Pittsburgh

The first time New Jersey Devils left winger Zach Parise skated in an NHL game came quite early in life. As an eight-year-old, Zach was chosen to escort one of the hometown Minnesota North Stars onto the ice at the team's season opener. And who was Zach's partner on ice? Derian Hatcher, who is still in the NHL with Philadelphia.

"It was 6-foot-5 Derian Hatcher and 4-foot-1 Zach!" laughed Zach's father, former NHLer J-P Parise. And while Hatcher literally overshadowed Parise that night, the story is being reversed very quickly these days.

Growing up in a hockey family, Zach caught the bug early in life. J-P remembers taking his son skating for the first time at age two.

"Like a good dad, I gave him a chair so he wouldn't fall over," J-P said. "He was done with that chair in four minutes."

As a child, Zach was constantly playing hockey with his brother, Jordan, who is 22 months older.

"We were always skating on the pond," Zach said. "Summer or winter we would always be on the ice." And when they weren't on the ice, Zach and Jordan were on rollerblades playing road hockey.

Naturally, being so close in age, Zach and Jordan were competitive with each other, but "nothing that would create fights," J-P said. "They would bump, but that's all."

Of course, when dad was away, those bumps could escalate.

"It was competitive, obviously," Zach recalled. "Me being the younger one, chances are when things get physical you're going to lose a lot. It usually ended with me crying and running away."

Jordan is a goalie in the New Jersey farm system, but J-P remembers trying to discourage him from the net position. Coaching a so-so summer team, J-P put his son up against one of the better squads to show him just what a goalie goes through.

"What does he do?" J-P said. "He gets a shutout. Over 35 shots."

That competitiveness runs in the family. J-P, who coached the boys several times over the years, remembers when he made the decision to tone it down a little.

"I was hard on them at first, and I felt terrible," he said. "I went home (one day) and thought, 'Why the heck am I doing this? This is supposed to be fun. I always had fun when I played hockey.' From then on, I would never yell at them. Players should look forward to the next game or practice."

And Zach did. He would go on to attend Shattuck-St. Mary's, a Minnesota prep school with a top-notch hockey program that also produced Sidney Crosby, Drew Stafford and Jonathan Toews. J-P has been a coach at SSM and is still director of prospect evaluation.

"In Minnesota, there's a rule that (public) high schools can play only, like, 30 games a year," Zach noted. "My dad's a smart guy. He knew we needed ice time to develop and at Shattuck you could play 70 games a year. We could be on the ice whenever we wanted and we had our own gym."

"Zach was an 'A' student," J-P said. "He even skipped a grade." Indeed, because Zach skipped Grade 7, J-P maintains the media has often mistakenly given 'youngest ever' accolades to other rising stars at SSM, forgetting Zach was putting up record numbers while playing one age bracket up.

While playing at SSM, Zach teamed up on a line with Ottawa Senators right winger Patrick Eaves and L.A. Kings prospect Brady Murray, son of NHL coach Andy Murray.

"I have to tell you, it was mighty fine," J-P said. "People would come out to see them."

Despite the fact that his dad was his coach, Zach doesn't recall being treated any differently by J-P, or the other players for that matter.

If J-P needed someone to demonstrate a drill for the team, he would tab Zach for the task, but the wise father always knew where to draw the line.

"We would never talk hockey to or from games," J-P revealed.

Even though Zach is now in the NHL, he still goes back to Shattuck in the summer to help his dad, work out at the school's facilities and even run practices with the bantam-level boys. Other alumni usually join him.

"You should see the scrimmages," J-P noted.

Growing up in Minnesota and having an ex-North Star as a father, it's no wonder Zach followed the path he did.

"We had pictures all around the house of him playing hockey and you know, you want to do what your dad did," Zach said. A different North Star, who was just beginning a Hall of Fame career at the time, served as another hockey hero—Mike Modano.

"He was the young stud in the NHL at the time, and being from Minnesota we all looked up to him," Zach recalled. "As I got older I also started to watch guys like Joe Sakic and Peter Forsberg. I was amazed at what they could do."

After Shattuck, Zach was a standout at the University of North Dakota and was highly ranked going into the 2003 draft. *The Hockey News* had him slotted 10th overall prior to the draft and Zach was excited.

"Of course you look through the magazines like *The Hockey News* and see where you're ranked," Zach said. "You've interviewed with teams, like, four or five times and think, 'That interview went really well.' "

But Zach wasn't picked 10th. And with each passing pick, he began to get more nervous.

"It got to the 12th pick, then 13th—my agent turned to me three or four times and said 'this has *got* to be the one,' " Zach remembered.

At that point, fate seemed to be smiling on Zach—the New York Islanders were picking 15th, and J-P had been a star on Long Island.

But the Isles ended up picking another second-generation NHLer, Robert Nilsson, son of Kent Nilsson. Both father and son Parise were stunned.

"I was surprised myself when the Islanders passed," J-P recalled. "I said, 'Oh my gosh, Zach's a better player than those guys.' "

Despite the drop, J-P reassured his son.

"He was disappointed," J-P said. "He's a proud kid. But I told him, 'When it's time to play, you'll be ready to play.' "

Zach was eventually taken 17th overall by perennial powerhouse New Jersey, which was just fine for dad.

"It's like a privilege," J-P said. "Your team is winning and you're making a contribution. If you get drafted high, it's a last-place team. This is not fun after a couple of weeks."

And J-P was right. In just his second NHL season, Zach burst onto the scene with a terrific Stanley Cup playoff performance, playing with rookie Travis Zajac and veteran Jamie Langenbrunner on a very effective scoring line for the Devils.

And as for that first time he hit NHL ice, way back when he was an eight-year-old holding Derian Hatcher's hand at the blueline? Zach said he still thinks about that, especially during the eight games a year his Devils play Hatcher's Flyers.

"He probably doesn't remember me," Zach said.

But with the speed Zach plays at now, it's safe to say the towering Philadelphia defenceman has seen the back of his jersey at least a couple times.

✦ DRILL *"I just shoot. Pour a bucket of pucks between the hash marks and shoot. Even in the summer, (shoot) every chance you get."*

– RK

Corey
Perry

From Sniper to Crasher

Born: May 16, 1985 – Peterborough, Ont.

First Team: Haileybury Beavers

Heroes: Joe Sakic, Wayne Gretzky, Mario Lemieux

NHL Debut: Oct. 5, 2005 at Chicago

When Anaheim Ducks sparkplug Corey Perry was nine years old, he and his family moved to the 'big city.' Which one, you ask? Peterborough, Ont.

Okay, so Peterborough—Corey's birthplace—isn't very big. But when you grow up in the town of Haileybury in northern Ontario (population 4,000), moving to Peterborough, a town with its own legendary major junior team, seems pretty sweet. And for a kid who was already laying waste to his local league up north, the change was welcome.

"When I was eight years old, I was playing an age group up," recalled Corey. "I scored 205 goals that year."

So yeah, goal scoring was never a problem. This was especially true in Haileybury, where the sparse population meant nearly every kid who tried out, even for the top team, usually made it.

"Corey was very laid back," said Geoff Perry, Corey's father. "He would pass the puck before shooting it, but a lot of the kids, it would bounce off their sticks." And with Corey's advanced skills came acrimony from fellow parents, especially since Geoff happened to be coaching his son that year.

"It was difficult," Geoff recalled. "There was a lot of resentment. 'Your kid's always on the ice,' that sort of thing."

Despite that, young Corey just stuck to what he did best and didn't worry about the politics. "Goal-scoring was huge for me back then," Corey said. "I just wanted to play every day."

Corey began skating at the age of two and played his first organized hockey when he was five. There was really only one path he ever considered following. "It came pretty naturally," Corey said of the sport. "I always had a stick, or a mini-stick, in my hands."

Geoff built a backyard rink for Corey and his brother, A.J., who is two years younger than Corey, to help the boys get as much practice as they could. Thanks to the chilly climate in Haileybury, the Perry brothers were able to do battle outside from October to March.

But as great as Haileybury was as a place to grow up, the hockey wasn't up to par for Corey's talents. "Hockey was huge there," Corey said. "But you had to leave town to play triple-A. Actually, you had to leave town even to play single-A."

Geoff had originally come to Haileybury as a rookie Ontario Provincial Police officer, but had roots in Peterborough, where his father had once been an OPP inspector. He had some contacts with the Peterborough Minor Petes organization and arranged a transfer as his boys tried out for elite teams in their respective age brackets. Usually kids are upset at the prospect of moving to a new town. The Perry boys were enthusiastic, Geoff recalled. "They were excited that they knew they had somewhere to play already," he noted.

The move also let Corey and A.J. watch the OHL's Petes up close and personal. "The Petes were obviously a huge thing," Corey recalled. "Every Thursday night was game night."

With the move completed, Corey picked up where he left off in Haileybury, leading the bantam triple-A Petes in scoring en route to a championship at the OHL Cup. "The competition there was really good," Corey said. "I was testing myself against (future NHLers) like Geoff Platt (Columbus), Brent Burns (Minnesota) and Anthony Stewart (Florida)."

After that excellent season, Corey was ready to play in the Ontario League—hopefully for his hometown Petes. Instead, the London Knights, who were on the verge of becoming a powerhouse, snapped Corey up in the OHL draft. Rick Nash was the rising superstar on the team, which had recently been purchased by former NHLers Mark and Dale Hunter.

"To me, that was a great thing to happen in Corey's life," Geoff said. "Mark and Dale knew the ins and outs of the hockey world."

The Knights were developing into an OHL power, but challenges lay ahead for Corey in his second year. Although Nash was drafted first overall by the Columbus Blue Jackets, everyone assumed he would be sent back to London for one more year of seasoning. Nash had other plans. Thanks to a fantastic training camp, Nash made the Columbus roster, leaving the Knights without their top gun and Corey as the one tabbed to pick up the slack.

"It put a big load on Corey's shoulders," Geoff said. "He struggled at first, but adjusted by Christmas. He had to learn to play a lot more minutes."

Corey learned to love those minutes, and his junior career continued to flourish. In his final year, Corey led a juggernaut Knights team that also featured Edmonton prospects Rob Schremp and Danny Syvret. He led the OHL in goals (47), assists (83) and points (130). Not only were the Knights nearly unbeatable, but the Memorial Cup just happened to be in London that year, setting up a showdown with the Quebec League's own powerhouse, the Sidney-Crosby-led Rimouski Oceanic. The two teams clashed in an all-time classic Memorial Cup opener.

"That first game against Rimouski was one of the highlights of my career," Corey said. "We were down 3-1 in the first 10 minutes, but we came back and won it in overtime."

If the first London-Rimouski tilt was the highlight, the rematch in the final may have been the lowlight. Despite an embarrassment of talent at the Cup, it was also the final year of the obstruction era, and games devolved into muggings and wrestling matches.

"The first shift of the final, I came out on the ice and someone sucker punched me," Corey noted. "I don't remember anything about that game. I've watched it three or four times on tape since, but I don't remember any of it."

But father Geoff wasn't surprised. "That whole season Corey was marked," he said. "I told him, 'You gotta earn your space out there. If someone whacks you across the ankle, you whack him across the ankles harder.'"

That lesson must have stuck, because in his short tenure with the Anaheim Ducks, Corey has established himself as a hard-nosed player who isn't afraid to bang around. It may be a far cry from his days as a 205-goal scorer, but it's paying off, as Corey has established himself as a player other teams don't like to play against. "When teams say that, it's a confidence booster," Corey said.

Along with fellow young stars Ryan Getzlaf and Dustin Penner, Corey formed the 'PPG Line' in Anaheim in 2006–07. Despite being the Ducks' second offensive unit, they played like a first line during the 2007 Stanley Cup championship run.

"Definitely in the playoffs, that's when we were clicking," Corey said. "We don't have that worry about winning the Cup, but we want to win more of them."

For father Geoff, seeing his boy grow up from a little-league sniper to a total player who already had a Stanley Cup ring after just two NHL seasons was surreal.

"It's something you dream about," Geoff said. "You think, 'Boy, we must have done something right with this individual.' "

What's ironic is that Corey had predicted his fate to his parents way back when he was five years old. "I told them one day I'd play for them on TV and win a Cup," Corey recalled. "And now I've done it."

 *"After practice I like to shoot pucks as if I were on the power play. I walk out from the half-boards and shoot from just above the slot. It's a great position."*

– RK

Dion
Phaneuf

The Calgary Cannon

Born:	April 10, 1985 – Edmonton, Alta.
First Team:	South West Area Two
Heroes:	Grew up cheering for the Edmonton Oilers
NHL Debut:	Oct. 5, 2005 at Minnesota

P aul Phaneuf loved hearing the sound of pucks thumping into the concrete walls of the basement in his Edmonton home. The sound of glass shattering, well that's a little different.

But that's the price you pay when your son is a phenom with a rocket of a slapshot.

The reason Calgary Flames defenceman Dion Phaneuf has such a blistering shot is simple: he worked on it constantly.

In the winter, he'd awake mornings before school and blast away on the backyard rink. At night, too, after the homework was done, and if he didn't have a game or practice to go to, he'd be on the rink again. In the summer, he'd be outside shooting into the net. Any other time, he'd be in the basement firing pucks off a sheet of plastic—coated with WD-40 oil to make it slicker—honing his skills.

The thrill for Paul was hearing his son's shot become stronger and stronger. The disappointment was the needed repairs.

"He knocked out about three or four windows, some even after I put hard wire in front of them," Paul recalled. "I didn't want to put plywood over the windows in the basement, because I wanted to have some light down there, but eventually I had to put on plywood."

Reminded of his window-crashing days, the Flames defenceman couldn't help but laugh.

"He put a lot of windows in that basement," Dion said. "I loved to shoot pucks every night and was lucky to have a basement to shoot in, but he had to do a lot of repairs."

Now, instead of windows bearing the brunt of Dion's blasts, it's NHL goaltenders. And the nets those goalies are trying to guard.

The Flames had big expectations of the 6-foot-3, 210-pound blueliner when they drafted him ninth overall in 2003. So far, he has exceeded them. In his first campaign, he became only the third rookie defenceman in NHL history to score 20 goals—the other two are Brian Leetch and Barry Beck—and he added 29 assists.

In 2006–07, Dion hit the 50-point barrier, with 17 goals and 33 assists. He has appeared in an NHL All-Star Game and won gold medals with Canada at the 2005 World Junior Championship and at the 2007 World Championship.

Not bad for that youngster who would ask his dad to come on the ice with him in the backyard and help him practise his one-timers.

"I'd like to take that credit, but that was him," Paul said. "He'd be out on the ice shooting pucks all the time. He would set up his own drills, going through the pylons and working on his skating. Actually, that's one good thing about a small, backyard rink—you're always turning. I think it made him a better skater.

"And then he'd ask me to come out and feed him for one-timers. I'd be out there a long time because he just wouldn't quit. I don't know how his arms held up. But, I guess it's like anything—you work hard over and over and perfect your technique."

By his best guess, Paul bought 30 to 50 pucks a year, enough to keep a couple of five-gallon buckets filled for those sessions.

Still, there is more to Dion's game than the booming slapshot.

He's already one of the most feared bodycheckers in the NHL. He has been the overwhelming choice as the league's hardest hitter in several player polls.

Like every young NHL defenceman, Dion is still developing his defensive-zone play; but, based on the work ethic he developed as a boy, it's hard to believe it won't be long before he starts fulfilling those Norris Trophy expectations.

"Dion lived and breathed hockey, no question, from a very early age. He was always out on the ice," his dad said. "He'd be out there skating in the morning before breakfast and could stay out until midnight if we'd have let him."

Still, Dion is the first to say there are plenty of others who deserve credit for where he's at today. "I had a lot of great coaches growing up," he said. "Minor hockey in Edmonton was great. It was a lot of fun."

But one bench boss tops his list: Red Deer Rebels owner/GM/coach Brent Sutter.

"Brent had a huge impact on me," said Dion, who was twice named the Western League's top defenceman. "In my four years in Red Deer, he taught me a lot of little things that make the game easier when you make the step to the next level.

"He always said he tries to run his organization as close to how a professional hockey team would be run as he could. When you make the next step, you see how he did that.

"I can't say how much he helped me."

Sure, Sutter is a demanding coach, but Dion knew all along every lesson, whether it was about eating a proper diet or maintaining fitness or making a proper breakout pass, was going to help him in the long run.

"It was more the lifestyle of trying to make yourself a professional hockey player," Dion said. "In practice, there were little things he would harp on and harp on and harp on. When you're younger, you wonder why he's putting so much emphasis on it—but when you make the step to the next level, you see it."

As focused and intense as Dion is—his stare reminds some of Mark Messier—he's a huge proponent of fun.

That was the goal, whether it was firing pucks in the basement, playing on the backyard rink with his buddies or even taking to the ice in those early years.

"My dad never coached me, but I can't say enough about how much my parents did for me growing up," he said of Paul and his mother, Amber. "Whether it be taking me to the rink for 6 a.m. practices or making a lot of sacrifices financially, they were there.

"Maybe they wouldn't take a trip just because I'd be in a hockey tournament that would cost a lot of money (for them to attend). They made a lot of sacrifices, time or money, for me to be in hockey."

As for those who think the secret to making the NHL is hard work, Dion sees it another way.

"I really just shot a lot of pucks and had fun with my buddies on the rink," he said. "It was always about having fun. When you take the fun out of it, you don't know what you're playing for."

✦ DRILL   *"Shoot as many pucks as you can. Growing up, I'd do it all the time. Just blast away and have a good time, that's the main thing. You'll learn to work on your technique."*
— Randy Sportak

Alexander
Radulov

Student of the Game

Born:	July 5, 1986 – Nizhni Tagil, Russia
First Team:	Sputnik
Heroes:	Sergei Fedorov, Alexander Mogilny, Wayne Gretzky, Valeri Kharlamov
NHL Debut:	Oct. 21, 2008 vs. Vancouver

Even as a boy, Alexander Radulov understood the importance of a good education. "In school, there wasn't much time to think about hockey," he said. "You have to learn and study."

The Nashville Predators right winger admits, though, that there were times during his youth when he focused all of his educational energies on one thing: hockey. "I tried to stay on the ice as much as possible," Alexander said. "Sometimes I missed school—I just went straight to the rink and skated with everyone, with every team they had there.

"I didn't listen to anybody who told me something about (anything other than) hockey—I am what I am in hockey because I just try to work hard."

Even though he now has established himself as an NHL player, his work ethic has not changed. His manic approach to learning the game has led him to the conclusion that he doesn't just want to find one thing that works and stick with it. He wants to know everything that has ever worked in the sport, why it has worked and how he can make it work for him—just like when he was a kid.

There's no telling what he knows about the history of the Russian Czars, but it seems there's no limit to what he knows about the history of the game and those who have played it. That much was evident to Terry Crisp, a three-time Stanley Cup winner (two as a player, one as a coach) and a Predators broadcaster, during a night in Minnesota shortly after Alexander joined the team.

Alexander sought out Crisp during an off night and, for the first of what turned out to be many discussions between the two, tried to syphon off as much information as possible.

"This kid is a blotter," Crisp said. "In the space of 10 minutes (that first night) he asked me about 800 questions. He knew players. He knew my background and my history. It's not just present-day players with him, he knew all about the old-timers too. His favourite expression is, 'What do you mean?' Then when you think you're finished and start to walk away he grabs you by the shoulder and says, 'Not done, not done.'

'One thing that strikes me is he wants to learn all aspects of it. He wants to fill a whole darn book about the game."

'The Collected Works of Alexander Radulov' began on that sheet of ice at the rink in his hometown of Nizhni Tagil, Russia. There, even as a seven- or eight-year-old, he shared time with teams of all age groups. Some of the players might have been twice his own age.

It continued at the knee of his father, Valery, a one-time defenceman who played professionally in Russia, and on the heels of older brother Igor, a forward who played 43 NHL games during parts of the 2002–03 and 2003–04 seasons. It even included time spent in front of the television each Saturday morning as he faithfully tuned into an NHL highlights program.

"When I was a kid I just skated with everyone...go out there on the ice and try to learn some things," he said. "They all knew me and they all knew my dad. I was just skating. I didn't do the drills with them—I tried not to mess around. If they played in one zone, I'd go in the other zone."

Long before he encountered Crisp, Alexander listened to all that his father had to say. Much of it focused on the ideas of work ethic and passion, two things that the young man took to heart.

"He said, 'If you feel that you're not working hard and you're not working 100 per cent, you'd better just get off the ice and go do something else because this is not the way (hockey) is,' " Alexander said.

"You have to work hard—it doesn't matter if it's practice or a morning skate or a game or you just go skate with some guys. You have to work hard all the time. He was always trying to teach me everything he could. I'm not afraid to say that if it wasn't for him, I don't think I would be that successful."

Alexander's time on skates rarely focused on any one aspect of the game. Often, he was at the mercy of someone else's practice sessions. Whatever the team on the ice at the time was doing, he watched and tried to mimic later.

One thing that time did allow for consistently was the opportunity to hone his shot.

"I'd shoot it at the wall, most of the time at the wall," he said. "Sometimes when the goalie had a break I'd come from the wing and shoot it. That was a fun time. It's fun to remember. You shoot at the blueline or some letter you see. When you're a little kid, that's all you need."

He did so because limitations of time and space offered few other opportunities at that point. However, it turned out to be the best thing he could do, which he eventually realized once he had studied the North American game.

"I learned that you have to shoot if you want to score," he said. "In Russia, everyone's deking and everything but (in North America) it's more shots and more straight-ahead games. I like it. You're not scoring if you're not shooting."

As a rookie in 2006–07, he was seventh in goal-scoring for Nashville with a franchise rookie-record 18 goals in 64 games. His shooting percentage (18.8) led a team that included the likes of Paul Kariya, Jason Arnott and J-P Dumont. That followed a record-setting junior career in Quebec, where he had 61 goals in 62 games as an 18-year-old. His success at an early age was the result of his single-mindedness in pursuing a career in hockey.

Yet within that approach he has been—and remains—completely open-minded in an attempt to learn anything and everything.

"I was a little kid and grew up in a small town, where many of us played hockey," he said. "There's nothing to do in my town except to go to school and to play hockey because it's cold. I skated outside, too—winter especially. It was a lot of fun when it's freezing outside—minus-25 or minus-30, it's still fun. When I was a kid I went everywhere. I played outside and skated in the snow. Everything in my life was hockey, and it's still hockey."

✦✦ TIP *"Work hard and be smart. All the time you are out on the ice, just work hard."*
— David Boclair

Mike
Richards

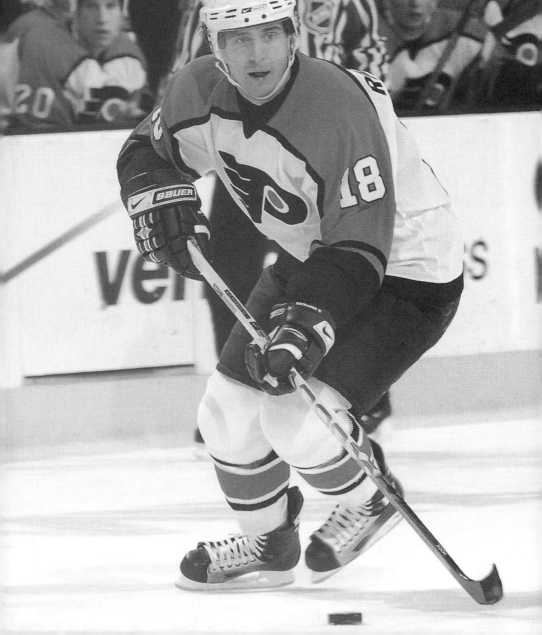

Long Rides to Glory

Born:	Feb. 11, 1985 – Kenora, Ont.
First Team:	Century Cinema Stars
Heroes:	Pavel Bure, Peter Forsberg
NHL Debut:	Oct. 5, 2005 vs. New York Rangers

Adjusting to major junior hockey is a big challenge for most every player who makes it to that level. The game moves faster, the competition gets bigger and the added expectations that go along with being one step from the big time can be crippling.

But for Mike Richards, one aspect of the jump to the Ontario League was no problem at all.

Growing up in the northwestern Ontario town of Kenora, with a population of 16,500, Mike was accustomed to lengthy bus trips. Playing major junior with the Kitchener Rangers certainly required him to elevate his game a notch, but it also meant spending a lot less time on highways.

"The OHL was a piece of cake," said the young centre, who was drafted 24th overall by the Philadelphia Flyers in the 2003 draft. "Fifteen minutes to Guelph, an hour to anywhere around Toronto, an hour to London. The longest (trip) was eight hours to Sault Ste. Marie and we only did that twice a year."

In bantam, his Kenora team (coached by his dad, Norm) played in a triple-A Manitoba league. The shortest trip they made was two hours to Winnipeg; the longest was 10 hours to Thompson in northern Manitoba.

Spending 10 hours on the bus might seem like a nightmare for some, but at the time, it was an excuse for fun with the boys.

"He probably said the most fun trip he had was to Thompson," said Irene Richards, Mike's mom. "I wouldn't go 10 hours on a bus – that doesn't interest me one little bit – but they would make makeshifts beds and I think they had a blast going up there."

Mike's first tangible steps toward the NHL began when his peewee coach, Barry Reynard, told then-Kitchener GM Jamie McDonald about Mike's skills. McDonald made the trip north to see Mike for himself and eventually selected him fourth overall in the 2001 Ontario League draft.

It was with the Rangers that Mike began building his reputation as a player with good all-around skills and great leadership qualities who simply knew how to win. He was Kitchener's leading scorer when the Rangers claimed the 2003 Memorial Cup. He was also named captain of a Canadian dream team that featured the likes of Sidney Crosby and Patrice Bergeron at the 2005 World Junior Championship. Again, Mike's team took the title. His first foray into professional hockey was with the American League's Philadelphia Phantoms and, sure enough, after his first playoff with the team Mike was hoisting the Calder Cup.

But before any of those triumphs had him in the spotlight, Mike began playing hockey as a five-year-old on an outdoor rink at Kenora's Evergreen Community Club. The Richards family, along with another family, helped run the club. Mike, his brothers, Matt and Mark, and his dad would help take care of the ice while Irene often worked at the concession stand. Mike's older cousin, Jeff Richards, was also a fixture on the ice and went on to blaze a path for Mike in the OHL by playing with the Sault Ste. Marie Greyhounds.

"We got out and made the ice, flooded the rink, took care of the community club and we just skated on the outdoor rinks," Mike recalled. "When we wanted to play we'd just take the key, grab a shovel and go."

According to Irene, Kenora had only one indoor rink at the time. That meant indoor ice time was at a premium.

"Access to indoor ice was (virtually) non-existent, so everybody kind of played outside," Irene said. "The outdoor rinks used to be just packed, so of course you had 25-year-olds, 20-year-olds, 15-year-olds. It was first come, first serve; you were there, you got to play."

Despite giving up several years, inches and pounds to most of the players on the ice, Mike was never afraid to enter the fray. His refusal to be deterred by bigger, better competition was probably an early clue as to why he is widely seen as future NHL captain material.

"Even as a 10-year-old, he played with anybody, it didn't matter who it was," Irene said. "And if there was nobody to play with, he'd just shoot the puck. So that was like our backyard, except it wasn't in our backyard, it was a few blocks away."

Some people feel exposure to high-level coaching and advanced drills are the best way for a hockey player to develop skills. Irene is convinced it was playing outdoors, where there were no whistles or coach's whiteboards, which helped Mike so much in his early days.

"It was the outdoor ice that, I'm going to say, really developed his skills because he wouldn't get that playing under watchful eyes all the time," she said. "He just went out there and had fun."

He still does. Mike might be paid handsomely for his services as a player now, but the driving force behind his desire to play is still rooted in the fact that it's simply an enjoyable thing to do.

That's why he's particularly frustrated when he finds himself in the stands at youth games and sees players and parents losing perspective on why they're there.

"It always seems like everybody is so intense at the games and it gets away from being fun," Mike said. "It frustrates me when you go to a rink and you see kids get mad on the ice. Really, when you're young it's all about fun, and even now I love playing the game. As long as you have that passion for the game and keep having fun you're going to want to do it.

"Parents yelling at their kids to do well on the ice isn't the way to go. My parents have been so good to me; they have never put pressure on me to do anything I didn't want to do and they always kept it fun for me. I think that's why I've had success, because I've always loved to play the game. They made it that way for me."

★ ★ TIP   *"Above all else, the game should be fun. Too many parents take the game too seriously when their kids are still very young. Going to the rink should always be something a young player looks forward to."*

– RD

Jordan Staal

Just Sign Me Up

Born:	Sept. 10, 1988 – Thunder Bay, Ont.
First Team:	MacDonald Fuels
Hero:	Todd Bertuzzi
NHL Debut:	Oct. 5, 2006 vs. Philadelphia

As far as Jordan Staal was concerned, making the NHL was never going to be a problem.

Not because he knew, as a youngster, that his size and skill would set him apart right from the very beginning. It's just that Jordan assumed the process for making the best hockey league in the world was fairly straight-forward.

"Every fall we'd sign up Eric and Marc, sign the boys up so they could go play hockey," said Henry Staal, who, along with wife, Linda, has raised four hockey-playing sons. "I don't know how old (Jordan) was, but he said, 'Dad, I'm going to play in the NHL.'

"I said, 'Well, yes, that's nice Jordan, but you don't just play in the NHL. You've got to make it.' And he said, 'Well, no, you could just sign me up.'"

Years later, with his big-league dreams having been fulfilled, Jordan chuckles when asked if he recalls his early thoughts on getting to the NHL.

"My dad's told me that story a few times," laughed the 6-foot-4, 215-pound Pittsburgh Penguins centre, who scored 29 goals in his first NHL season. "Now that I've made it, it's kind of ironic."

Jordan, of course, wasn't the first member of his family to reach the NHL ranks. His oldest brother, Eric, blazed the path from the family's home just outside of Thunder Bay, Ont., to the bright lights of the big stage. The big centre, who is four years older than Jordan, won a Stanley Cup in just his second year with the Carolina Hurricanes. Marc, a defenceman who is almost two years older than Jordan, won two World Junior Championship titles with Canada.

But even with a couple of stars preceding him in the bloodline, Jordan managed to stand out right away. Especially when he stood up.

Ian Swalucynski coached Eric and Marc before Jordan, as well as the youngest Staal brother, Jared, who is two years younger than Jordan.

He pointed to one thing that distinguished Jordan from the rest.

"His sheer size," said Swalucynski, who coached Jordan as a peewee, bantam and minor midget player in Thunder Bay. "In my office I've got a picture of Eric at 13 and another of Jordan at 13 and Eric looks like he's about 10 and Jordan looks like he's about 15."

According to Swalucynski, there were other players who surpassed Jordan's talent, but none of them had the wingspan to go with it.

"He had a real advantage over kids because he was so big and so skilled," the coach said. "There were guys who were better than him that we played against, but his size and reach and determination set him apart."

Henry saw it too, noting it took a few years for Eric's talents to surface, whereas Jordan's jumped out instantly.

"I don't want to say Eric wasn't good, but he just never had that size Jordan had, that natural size that, by default, he couldn't help but be dominant," the proud father said.

As a peewee player at the age of 12, Jordan began skating for teams in Thunder Bay, an Ontario-based city of 120,000 on the northwest shores of Lake Superior. From there he followed Eric's footsteps to Peterborough, where he helped the Petes win an Ontario League championship in 2006 before Pittsburgh drafted him second overall that summer.

But his first strides toward the big time came outside Thunder Bay in the township of Oliver Paipoonge as a novice and atom player. Henry recalled some of the first indications he saw that there were competitive fires burning inside Jordan. One of them was during an atom tournament one week after Jordan's squad had fallen short at another event.

"We had our little country team and Jordan was sort of the star of the team," Henry said. "When we (hosted a tournament) at our rink, we made it to the final and I don't even know if Jordan scored and he was so upset because he thought the team really depended on him and he didn't score and they lost the game and he was almost in tears on the bench.

"And the next weekend we played the same bunch of teams (at a different tournament). We went to the final again and I think Jordan got seven goals and one assist and we won 8-1 or something like that. It was like he just said, 'OK, that's it, I'm not letting this happen again.'"

Jordan, who led the NHL with seven shorthanded goals as a rookie, also began giving some hints he might be a special penalty-killer. Allan Konopski coached Jordan when he was nine years old on an atom team comprised of 10- and 11-year-olds. When the team took a pair of penalties one game, Konopski wanted to send Jordan on the ice to kill off the 5-on-3 power play, but the youngster wasn't quite so sure he was the right player for the job.

"Our second or third game, we had two men in the penalty box and I was going to send Jordan Staal out to be the only forward with two defencemen to kill the penalty and Jordan said to me, 'Mr. K, I'm too young—I'm only nine years old,' " Konopski recalled. "I said 'Jordan, go out there and do your best and I'm sure you'll do fine.'

"Jordan went out there (for the full minute of the first penalty-killing shift) and killed the penalty and when he came back to the bench he was so happy."

Of course, much of Jordan's development occurred on the Staal family's backyard rink, which is rapidly becoming part of Canadian hockey lore.

"It was definitely fun (on the backyard rink) to go out and play with your friends," Jordan said. "We invited a lot of people over to our house."

As often happens when a bunch of boys get together, tempers sometimes ran a little hot.

"There were a few elbows thrown and sticks and stuff like that," recalled Jordan with a smile. "Some heated battles my mother had to take care of."

Whether the boys were aware of it or not, there was also a lot of learning going on. Trying to keep the puck away from three, five, even nine or ten prying sticks all at once is no small task.

"I think all four of us, we really learned how to use our bodies to fend away defenders," Jordan said. "We obviously couldn't (bodycheck) each other out there, so we had to use our bodies to get in front of people and I think that really helped the way we're able to protect the puck down low and walk out from corners."

The backyard rink certainly was a place to craft and hone those skills that would eventually take him to the NHL, even if it never felt like practice to Jordan and his brothers.

"It wasn't hard to get them out there," said Henry of his four sons, "but getting them back in at times was a different story."

"Ever since the time I could stand I had a hockey stick in my hand," Jordan said. "We lived and breathed it. For (the NHL dream) to come true, it's unbelievable."

✦ DRILL *"A hard, accurate shot is one of the best attributes a player can have. Shoot lots of pucks to build up wrist strength and work on your accuracy."*

– RD

Paul
Stastny

Family Dynasty

Born: Dec 27, 1985 – Quebec City, Que.

First Team: New Jersey Devils' youth team

Heroes: Peter Stastny, Joe Sakic, Peter Forsberg

NHL Debut: Oct. 4, 2006 vs. Dallas

Paul Stastny is so naturally strong that his older brother can't help but look at him with a tinge of good-natured envy. "I have to work my (butt) off to stay in hockey shape, and so does he, but just look at how strong he is naturally," said Yan Stastny, a centre in the St. Louis Blues' system.

With a Hall of Fame father in Peter Stastny, and two uncles—Marian and Anton—with NHL pedigree, Paul was around a lot of elite-level talent growing up. Undoubtedly the 6-foot, 210-pound Colorado Avalanche centre inherited a few choice genes. But, if he wanted to play hockey like they did, his dad made sure he was doing it for the right reasons.

That is, to be driven by the love and enjoyment of the game, rather than by an obsession to 'make it to the pros.'

"My dad never put pressure on us playing hockey," Paul recalled. "He wanted us to have fun, and that's really a big key to my development. Plus, with my dad and his European background, it wasn't just hockey growing up. In the summertime, he'd keep us off the ice and we'd play tennis and soccer and just run."

"But—" he added, "hockey's just in the blood."

Paul has been having fun at playing the game since he was five years old skating on Quebec City ponds when his dad was still a scoring machine for the Nordiques. Peter fled his native Czechoslovakia in 1980 to star in the NHL, where he would go on to score 450 goals and 1,239 points in 16 NHL seasons with Quebec, New Jersey and St. Louis.

"When Paul was still real young, Peter looked at him and would say, 'He is really something special,' " recalled Paul's mom, Darina. "Back then he loved to play outside, and he was always carrying his stick around, always playing. He just had good hockey sense that you can't teach."

Throughout the years, Darina would bolster that hockey sense where she could. She'd lay into her son when she saw him coasting or when he'd get caught conspicuously out of position. "Move your feet! Keep your feet moving, Paul!" was one of her favourite refrains.

"But (my parents) are both competitive spirits, and the main thing they wanted was for us to work hard, to give 100 per cent, and to have fun," Paul said.

Paul began playing organized youth hockey in New Jersey, when his dad was traded to the Devils in 1990. Though he doesn't remember his first goal in the Devils' youth organization, his mother does.

"In mites, when Paul scored that first goal, instead of celebrating with his teammates he skated right over to where I was seated and screamed, 'Mommy, Mommy, did you see that? I scored a goal!' He was just so cute," Darina remembered. (Paul doesn't like being called *cute*, but that's a mother's prerogative.)

In those years, Darina and Peter would switch off taking Paul and Yan to practice at 6 a.m. "If dad was off working, my mom would get up and take me," Paul said. "If they were both at home, dad was usually watching stocks on CNN or reading the *Wall Street Journal* in those early mornings, but he'd take me."

"Paul would always be the first one up," Darina remembered. "He was so excited to get to the rink."

Paul would go on to play club hockey for a few years when the family moved to St. Louis. He still laments letting his team down with a game against a first-place club one season when he was 11 years old.

"We always had those afternoon-type games," Paul recalled. "And one time I thought the game was at 3:45 p.m., but it turned out it had started at 2:45. I showed up at the rink to get suited up and my team came into the

locker room with their heads down. They were just soaked. I asked one of the guys what was going on, and he said, 'We just lost 5-4, where the heck were you?' I'd missed the game, and felt so bad that we nearly beat them anyway, and I could have made the difference. My mom was still parking the car, and I had to break the news to her."

By the time Paul reached Chaminade College Preparatory and Jr. B-level hockey in St. Louis, at age 14, he was showing signs of being a "special" player.

Darina thinks summer-league roller hockey helped bring along some of his more technical gifts. "Paul developed a lot of his stick-handling ability while playing roller hockey in the summers," she recalled. "He was an excellent roller hockey player and it really helped him become stronger."

Paul also continued to hone his hockey sense. He learned to read a play as it was developing, to compensate for his lack of speed with smart positional discipline, and to demonstrate strength with the puck, the hallmarks of his game in the NHL.

"I have never been the fastest guy, or the hardest-shooting guy, but at that point I began playing against older guys who were a lot quicker and stronger, and that was a big change," he said.

By the time he was playing in junior with the Omaha, Neb.-based River City Lancers of the United States League, Stastny was not considered a blue-chip prospect for his birth year of 1985 because he lacked obvious speed. But Lancers coach Mike Hastings was quick to point out to recruiting coaches such as Seth Appert at the University of Denver that the more you watch him, the more you appreciate his skills.

"The most prevalent comment on Stastny at that point was that he lacked speed, but his stick skill and hockey intelligence was good," recalled

Appert, now the coach at RPI. "And it's true—the more you were around him the more you realized how complete he was in all situations. He's just very detailed in his preparation and in how he approaches the game."

While at the University of Denver, Appert remembers the breakout moment when Paul got acclimated to the speed of that level and his instincts took over.

"We were playing Minnesota his freshman year and his dad was in the stands. We weren't sure how he'd respond to that and he'd struggled the first dozen games or so. But he scored three goals that weekend and we knew that he'd arrived," Appert said. "We went on to win the national title and he was a big part of that."

Appert says one of the big reasons for that is attitude. "Paul plays the game with a great level of maturity and he's fun to be around. He is very passionate about hockey, but not overly consumed with it."

There's no disagreement from Paul, who adds it's important to just be yourself.

"People will sometimes say, 'Oh, your uncle had that in his game' or, 'Your dad had that,' and it's good to be compared to more than one guy, but I never compare myself to anyone." Paul said. "I'm my own self."

Few players have had rookie seasons that could compare with Paul's 28-goal and 78-point rookie campaign with the Avalanche, a pleasant surprise for Colorado, which selected him 44th overall in 2005.

"Paul, he's a beauty," Yan said.

✦ **DRILL** *"You learn a lot in game-like situations. Flow drills, where you're skating and moving the puck and it ends in a 3-on-2, really help in learning the game. Moving the puck around and moving your feet, and simulating game-like situations."*
— Chuck Mindenhall

Alex
Steen

Born to Shoot

Born:	March 1, 1984 – Winnipeg, Man.
First Team:	River Heights Cardinals
Heroes:	Thomas Steen, Alex Zhamnov, Pavel Bure, Steve Yzerman
NHL Debut:	Oct. 5, 2005 vs. Ottawa

Hockey fanatics will tell you that the sport is their life, but Toronto Maple Leafs centre Alex Steen has the pedigree to back it up.

As the son of former Winnipeg Jets great Thomas Steen, Alex was practically raised on the ice. He started skating at two and spent his youth running around the rink while his famous Swedish father helped pave the way for generations of European players to come.

Even as a young child, Alex's passion was clear.

"He never played with regular toys," Thomas recalled. "All he ever played with was a hockey stick. He'd shoot tennis balls into the fireplace."

NHL legend and former Winnipeg Jets GM John Ferguson has known Alex since he was born.

"Every Christmas we used to invite the players over for a get-together," Ferguson said. "And he'd show up with his mini-stick and shoot balls around and I'd play with him."

Alex and his friend Craig Carlyle, son of former Jets defenceman Randy Carlyle, would play street hockey behind Winnipeg Arena and floor hockey outside the Jets' dressing room during games. Kids attending Jets games knew the pair would be there and often joined. And if he wasn't at the arena, Alex would still try to scare up a game.

"I'd grab some guys from our street and we'd go play another street on the pond," Alex recalled. "Just shovel off the snow and go. It's bragging rights."

As Alex got older his love of the game kept growing, something greatly aided by his access to some of the most talented Winnipeg teams ever.

"The guys were real good, they were all really nice," Alex said. "I especially remember the last years, which were some of the best: Teemu Selanne, Alexei Zhamnov, Keith Tkachuk, Nikolai Khabibulin. I'd skate on the ice after practice and shoot on the goalies sometimes."

Along with Craig, Alex played hockey with several other NHLers and top prospects. When Andy Murray came to Winnipeg to be an assistant coach, he added another talented kid to the mix: his son Brady Murray. Brady is a Los Angeles Kings prospect.

The three families teamed up when the boys were nine-years-old to form a powerful youth team.

"We were a tight-knit group of guys growing up," Alex recalled. "We were all on the same triple-A summer team together with Whitey—Ian White (now Alex's teammate in Toronto). Nigel Dawes of the Rangers was on that team, too."

Considering Thomas is a scout with the Minnesota Wild and Randy Carlyle and Andy Murray are coaches in the big league, it's safe to say the team had plenty of strong guidance.

"We had NHL coaches when we were 10 or 11, and we didn't even know it!" Alex laughed.

Thomas also remembers those wonderful times.

"It was so much fun," he said. "We went all over the place for three years — Toronto, Vancouver, Montreal, Detroit, Minneapolis."

The only problem was that the summer league started just after the Jets' playoff run ended, so Thomas's competitive juices weren't just flowing, they were gushing.

"I was still in NHL-playoff mode. I left the Winnipeg dressing room and the next week I'm in Vancouver with nine-year-olds," Thomas chuckled. "I didn't adjust so well. We won, but I was pushing the kids like an NHL team."

Unfortunately, the good times didn't last forever.

In 1996, the Winnipeg Jets were sold and moved to Arizona, where they became the Phoenix Coyotes. Thomas, who was nearing the end of his career, didn't want to move his family down south and decided to retire instead.

He wanted his sons—Alex's younger brother Hamilton was drafted in 2006 by the Western League's Red Deer Rebels—to continue playing hockey at an elite level and didn't think they could do that in Phoenix at the time, so the family moved to Germany.

After playing a handful of games in Frankfurt in 1996, Thomas got a call from the Berlin Polar Bears, which became his team for the next three seasons. The transition was tough for 12-year-old Alex, who had lived in Canada his whole life.

"It was nerve-wracking," Alex remembered. "I got thrown into a German school and had to learn the language. I had to read German all of a sudden."

In the end, however, Alex looks back on the experience positively.

"It's kind of an adventure," he said. "Now I speak fluent German."

At 15, Alex moved back to Sweden to play in the junior program. He played for Vastra Frolunda, in Gothenburg. Again, he had to adjust to another school system and another language.

"Culturally it wasn't that big an adjustment," said Alex, who spent many a summer in his homeland. "But in school—I had never written or read in Swedish." Even playing the game he loved was a bit different.

"Hockey-wise it was difficult, too," Alex said. "And not just because of the change in ice surface (it's bigger in Europe). Canadians seem to have more intensity in their bodies at that age, so it's more physical. But in Europe, the players seem to develop skills faster. Everyone sees the ice really well at that age."

Despite the adjustment, Alex played well enough at 17 to earn a promotion to Sweden's version of the NHL: the Elite League.

This was a big surprise for Alex's dad, who was scouting in Europe at the time.

"He was still too tiny to play with men," Thomas said. "They threw him in a game and I almost had a heart attack."

But to his father's relief, Alex hit a growth spurt that summer and the next season, he no longer had to look up at his opponents.

"He grew from boy to a little man in four months," Thomas noted. And when Alex started scoring at 18 (he had five goals and 15 points in 45 games), Thomas knew the NHL was a good possibility.

"It was not until then that you could see he had a chance."

The Maple Leafs had drafted Alex in the first round, 24th overall the previous season, and in 2005, he made his NHL debut. That was another surprise for Thomas, who thought his son would spend some time with the farm team first.

"That's the toughest step," Thomas noted. "Getting to the NHL."

And while Alex had a tough goalless streak at the beginning of his sophomore season, he became one of the team's best young stars. Many experts can tell he's got a lot to offer in the league.

"He's got the head smarts, ice smarts and vision on the ice," said Ferguson, who worked for the Sharks when Alex was drafted. "We wanted him in San Jose, I'll tell you.

"He's absolutely like his father—same expressions. Even today he moves the same way on the ice."

Ferguson remembered bumping into Alex when he was captaining Sweden at the 2003 World Junior Championship in Halifax. They hadn't seen each other in years, but the young star was as humble as ever.

"He came up to me and said, 'Mr. Ferguson, I'm Alex Steen.' " Ferguson recalled with a laugh. "I said, 'I know you are.' "

The whole hockey world knows him now, too.

✦ DRILL *"Set up some pylons and stickhandle through them while trying not to look at the puck, then pick a spot in the net and shoot at it. Eventually, you should be able to keep your head up the whole time and shoot the puck right where you want it."*

– RK

Ole-Kristian
Tollefsen

The Norwegian Monster

Born: March 29, 1984 – Oslo, Norway

First Team: Nes. I.K

Hero: Nicklas Lidstrom

NHL Debut: Nov. 23, 2005 vs. Nashville

Most NHL players have at least one thing in common: the life they're leading now is one they've been dreaming of since they first could hold a stick.

But when Ole-Kristian Tollefsen began playing hockey in Norway, his country had produced just one NHLer and his hometown had just completed building a roof over its lone arena.

Ole, a hard-nosed Columbus Blue Jackets defenceman, wasn't lured onto the ice after watching Wayne Gretzky or Mario Lemieux lift the Stanley Cup, but rather by a friend from school who kept talking about how much he enjoyed skating.

"There was a buddy of mine who got into skating school and he talked about it all the time and I thought, 'I want to try it, too,'" said Ole, who grew up in Mef, a town of about 7,000 located on the outskirts of Oslo.

Hockey certainly wasn't the first sport of choice for many kids growing up in Norway. When Ole started playing, the only player the country had ever sent to the NHL was Bjorn Skaare, who played one game for the Detroit Red Wings in 1978–79.

But Ole's dad, Ola, and his mom, Grethe, were both interested in sports and decided to support their son's decision to strap on the blades when he was seven years old. Ole's timing was terrific, as Mef's first indoor rink had just recently been constructed when he decided to hit the ice.

"We could just go there almost every day and just skate and do all the stuff we wanted," said Ole, who started playing organized hockey one year after he learned to skate. "It's a small (town) and we got all the ice time in the world if we wanted it."

While there were certainly enough kids interested in hockey to form youth teams, Ole and his young friends didn't spend much time chatting about their favourite NHL teams. The bright lights of the North American game didn't reach their corner of the world.

"We never heard about the NHL when we were that young," Ole said. "We started collecting hockey cards when we were, like, 12 or 13. That's when I maybe started thinking about it a little bit."

Ole may not have had much exposure to the NHL as a youngster, but he did have one unique hockey experience most North American fans can only dream of. When Norway played host to the 1994 Winter Olympics, a nine-year-old Ole and his family headed to Lillehammer to watch the likes of Paul Kariya and Peter Forsberg represent their respective countries on one of sport's biggest stages.

A few years later, at age 16, Lillehammer became home for Ole as he made the first big move of his hockey career. Competing for NGG Lillehammer in Norway's junior league, Ole would wake up, work out, go to school and then play hockey in the evenings. It was there he initially crossed paths with Patrick Thoresen, a future friend and teammate who blazed a path to North America and major junior hockey for Ole.

But before they ever played together on Norwegian national junior teams, Ole and Patrick, a forward, went toe-to-toe in search of a junior title. Even at that time, Ole was already exhibiting the aggressive, physical play that has become his hallmark in the NHL.

"I remember we met his team in the final when we played in junior," said Patrick, who played for Storhamar at the time and suited up for the Edmonton Oilers in 2006–07. "There were always a lot of tough battles around the net and in the corners, and he really focused on playing hard and trying to scare off the other opponents. He was always a tough guy to beat."

And since his team worked so hard to defeat Ole's Lillehammer crew in that showdown, Patrick still likes to make sure his buddy remembers who came out on top.

"He still gets to hear about that now," he chuckled.

Patrick may laugh now when recalling his victory, but when Ole made the leap from junior to the Norwegian Elite League at 17, nobody enjoyed playing against him. Patrick, who also played in the Elite League as a teenager, said Ole stood out because of his crunching hits and the fact that he wasn't yet old enough to take off his full-cage facemask.

"You couldn't take it off until you were 18, so we were both playing with full cages (on different teams) and I remember people talking about this crazy guy from Lillehammer, saying he was skating and playing so hard and he doesn't care about anything, he just wants to make it forward in the world," Patrick said. "He made some highlights early in Norway, and he really made a name for himself in that league and showed he could play men's hockey."

For his part, Ole has always enjoyed the physical element of hockey. Even from the time he first put on a pair of skates.

"I was always told, 'You've got to keep your head up' because I would always run into guys," he laughed. "I loved doing that when I was younger, too. It's always kind of been my nature."

Eventually Patrick and Ole became teammates, representing Norway at the 2002 World Junior Championship in the Czech Republic.

"He always brought a lot of toughness to the team," Patrick said. "He was one of those guys that stepped it up against those bigger nations. If we were playing Canada, he would have been one of the guys who stepped it up."

It was at that tournament that Ole began contemplating a move to North America and major junior hockey. Patrick, one year older than Ole, already played in the Quebec League at that time and Ole began questioning him about playing hockey abroad. People on this side of the ocean had similar thoughts.

"I asked (Patrick) a bit about playing in Canada and I played world juniors and all the agents came up to me and asked if I wanted to play and there were a couple of (major junior) scouts there, too," Ole said. "I guess I just decided if I got drafted that year, I wanted to go play junior, too. (Then) as soon as I got drafted I was like, 'I've got to make this choice now.' "

Playing for the Brandon Wheat Kings of the Western League may have been a good move for Ole, but that doesn't mean it wasn't an adjustment.

"It was a shock," said Ole of his initial days on Manitoba's prairies. "I didn't know what to expect because I didn't know anything about Brandon at all. I knew they had a good hockey team and it would be a good place to play, but I was surprised when I showed up there and the shortest bus trip was four hours (long). But it was a good place to play."

Now that he's cracked the big show, Ole wants to make sure youth-hockey players in Norway today don't have to depend on hockey cards to learn about the NHL the way he had to. Every summer, he and Patrick return home to help grow the game, which is becoming more popular, through hockey schools.

"There's more media attention about it with me and Patrick over here playing," Ole said. "It's helped out the sport for sure and hopefully we can bring more kids over and hopefully they can make it."

"Enjoy what your doing. Spending long hours on the ice won't seem like work if you truly enjoy all the different parts of the game."

– RD

Thomas
Vanek

International Man of Mystery

Born:	Jan. 19, 1984 – Graz, Austria
First Team:	Zell Am See
Heroes:	Jaromir Jagr, Mario Lemieux
NHL Debut:	Oct. 5, 2005 vs. N.Y. Islanders

When Thomas Vanek first came to North America, there was skepticism an Austrian could play elite-level hockey. Thomas himself will be the first to tell you his homeland is much better known for skiing than it is for skating, but that's something at which the Buffalo Sabres sniper has become quite adept. In fact, he has proven himself at every level.

"I still remember in the playoffs, he got the puck on the off-wing," said Bob Motzko, who coached a 15-year-old Thomas with Sioux Falls of the United States League, then later at the University of Minnesota. "He was breaking down the zone. Our whole bench leaned forward—the crowd, too. We all took a breath, wondering 'What's going to happen next?' There was always an anticipation.

"Of course, he scored on the guy."

It was his obvious skill that made believers out of many in the U.S. Midwest, where Thomas would play three seasons with the Stampede before becoming a star Golden Gopher.

"Some guys were jealous when he came in, because he was taking a roster spot away (from a North American player)," recalled Sioux Falls teammate and Carolina Hurricanes winger Chad LaRose. "But once they saw him play it was like, 'Wow, this guy can really play the game.'"

Thomas grew up in Vienna, the capital of Austria, where his Czech-born father, Zdenek Vanek, played for Zell Am See of the Austrian League.

"I remember hanging around him at the rink and loving the game," Thomas said.

And although catching NHL games on Austrian TV was difficult because of the time difference, Thomas remembers watching a one-hour hockey-magazine show every week, where he would catch up on the exploits of his childhood heroes, Mario Lemieux and Jaromir Jagr.

"Back then, the Penguins were the best," Thomas recalled. "Jagr, he was one of the biggest stars in Europe. He still is."

Thomas first started playing at age four, in the Zell Am See feeder system. As he got older, the team traveled all over Europe for tournaments in places like Germany, the Czech Republic and Slovenia.

He would also get his first taste of North American hockey while playing in a peewee tournament in Quebec. That's when he began to think of a relocation that would change his life forever.

At 14, Thomas decided he was going to move to Canada. His father had a contact in Lacombe, Alta., outside of Red Deer, so that's where Thomas headed.

"At 14, it wasn't an easy decision," Thomas said. "It was a lot better level of hockey and you don't want that opportunity to go away."

Despite his young age, Thomas said his parents were behind him all the way. "They said, 'Go and try it, and if it doesn't work out, you can always come home.'"

And although the wilds of Alberta were far from big city Vienna, Thomas thrived in an atmosphere where everything was hockey.

"Just seeing how many kids played hockey was great," he said.

After a year in Lacombe, Thomas was to join a team in Rochester, N.Y., but the team ran into some troubles and didn't have the resources to support him.

"They couldn't take care of him, what with the schooling and housing," Motzko noted. Instead, Thomas was hooked up with Motzko, who was due to coach a brand-new junior team in Sioux Falls.

"Lucky phone call," Motzko chuckled.

Not only was Thomas in a stable environment once again, he was also in an exciting one.

"I thought it was awesome," Chad remembered. "It was their inaugural season, so we were playing in front of like, 5,000 people."

Thomas attended high school in Sioux Falls and continued to make the adjustment to life in North America.

"He spoke three languages and picked up English very quickly," Motzko said. "He really handled that well."

Not that it was a seamless transition.

"The hockey was always fun and I could relate to guys on the ice, but off the ice it was tough," Thomas recalled. "It took two or three months to understand most of it (English)."

When he did pick up all the subtleties of the language, Thomas became just another one of the guys, albeit one who spoke a bit differently.

"We had a pretty loose group of guys and once he got loose, he was a pretty goofy guy," Chad said. "The guys loved him. He'd crack jokes with his little accent."

The team would also go on road trips, which Chad said worked as great bonding sessions. Although most of their opponents were close to their South Dakota home base, the Stampede would travel to Ann Arbor, Mich. to take on the U.S. national team development program. On the way back from one of those trips, the team also had a game in Chicago and took in a Blackhawks game.

If there was one thing Thomas really noticed about North America, it was the food. Back in Austria, he said, home cooking is much bigger than fast food, so seeing the Golden Arches everywhere was an eye-opener.

"I couldn't believe how many McDonald's you would pass between school and the rink," Vanek recalled. "In Austria, a city of 250,000 people might have two."

In the end, Thomas' stellar play in Sioux Falls landed him a spot with the famous Minnesota Golden Gophers, where he would play two seasons and be named MVP of the 2003 NCAA championship tournament.

Thomas was taken fifth overall in the 2003 draft by Buffalo and his play through two seasons made him by far the most prominent Austrian in the NHL.

But the boy from Vienna hasn't forgotten about his native land. He still goes back in the summer for three weeks and is always touting the latest talent coming out of Austria.

"More and more kids are coming over," he said. "Vancouver picked an Austrian 14th at the 2006 draft (Michael Grabner), Philadelphia picked another one (Andreas Nodl, 39th overall), so it's growing."

If the next wave of Austrian prospects has the same talent that Thomas has brought to the table in his young career, NHL scouts may want to head over there more often.

"He's not a lazy player. He's very smart," Motzko said. "(Critics) said he wasn't playing defence, but look at his plus-minus (plus-47 in 2006–07). That's what he'll do—he'll take challenges."

And Motzko has no doubt his former charge can take on those challenges when an important game is on the line.

"The bigger the stage, the bigger he plays."

 *"Work hard on your shooting, and practise picking corners. Above all else, always put your team first."*

-RK

Cam
Ward

Making the Right Move

Born:	Feb. 29, 1984 – Saskatoon, Sask.
First Team:	Saskatoon Flyers
Hero:	Curtis Joseph
NHL Debut:	Oct. 5, 2005 at Tampa Bay

Ken Ward had visions of capturing, on video, his young son charging up the ice to score a coast-to-coast goal. But the little guy just didn't want to do his part.

"When Cameron was playing entry-level hockey, I remember video taping (a game)," said Ken, father of Carolina Hurricanes goalie Cam Ward. "All the players rotated playing goal (during the game) and he was running to his coach just begging to be the goalie all the time, and I made a comment on the video, unwittingly, that it was kind of a waste of tape because all he was going to do was stand there in net."

Years later, it's pretty clear Cam was on to something. But how was his dad supposed to know he'd not only go on to be a goalie, but win the Conn Smythe Trophy as playoff MVP in his rookie season as well?

"I was trying to encourage him to go and do something while I (was taping him play)—make a rush or something, because he always skated extremely well," Ken explained.

In truth, Ken also had a big hand in Cam wanting to play goal. Ken played the position himself in oldtimer leagues and that's part of what compelled Cam to put on the pads.

"My dad was a goaltender, too, and for some reason I immediately wanted to be a goalie, even though in minor hockey, in those days, you just took a turn as goalie and the goalie didn't wear any equipment," said Cam, who played three years under coach Brent Sutter with the Western League's Red Deer Rebels before moving on to the big league.

When he wasn't standing in front of pucks, his strong skating helped make Cam a superb defenceman while playing novice hockey in Saskatoon. There was also a lot of hockey played inside the Ward home. An unfinished basement provided the perfect forum. Cam's younger sister, Chelsea, is a hockey player herself and Cam said she could hold her own in any road hockey game when they were kids.

Ken got involved in the basement battles, too.

"We'd always go down there and put goal nets up at either end of the basement and just have games against each other," Ken said.

One summer, while the Wards were in the process of moving to Winnipeg, Cam was asked to be part of a select summer team based in Brandon, Man., which was traveling to Edmonton for the prestigious Brick Invitational Tournament.

There was no doubt Cam, who was playing both defence and goal at the time, wanted to take part. But he did have a decision to make.

"I said to him, 'Okay, you have one choice: you either try out as a goaltender or you try out as a defenceman,'" Ken recalled. "He said, 'I want to try out as a goaltender.' In retrospect, it was the smartest thing he ever did."

Ken believes Cam's decision to move to the crease not only helped him make the most of his skills, but it also helped remove Cam from any scenario where favouritism could enter into the equation when he was fighting for a spot on a team.

"It's truly the one position that the politics of the sport are not allowed to impact decisions, because if you're clearly better than the other little kid standing in goal, it's obvious," he said.

While living in Winnipeg, Cam made the commitment to playing goal full-time. But his early days as a defenceman still served as a benefit, as did his strong skating stride.

"People underestimate the skating ability of a goaltender," Cam said. "You've got to be a good skater so you can have good mobility.

"It's not always about standing in goal and dropping to your knees. For rebounds, you've got to have good, quick mobility to be able to get up and react."

It was while playing in Winnipeg that Cam crossed paths with another future NHLer, Alex Steen of the Toronto Maple Leafs. The two never played on the same squad, but saw plenty of each other playing in the same atom league. Steen's father, Thomas, was playing for the NHL's Jets at the time and told Ken, after seeing Cam, that he felt the young stopper had the game to go far in hockey. As fate would have it, Cam was eventually selected 25th overall in the 2002 NHL draft, one spot after Alex.

The next family move presented a challenge for Cam. When he was a peewee goalie, his family picked up and headed west to the Edmonton suburb of Sherwood Park. Cam, anxious to start playing with a new set of teammates, was disappointed to find out the town's top peewee squad already had its tender tagged.

"The year we moved there I came in a little late and actually got stuck down playing peewee A," Cam said. "The top team is peewee AA, but they had already chosen their goalie, so I was a little bit too late."

Undaunted, Cam played in a league that was likely below his skill level at the time before returning to the appropriate level the next year.

While in Sherwood Park, Cam had the opportunity to see his craft performed at the highest level.

"I was always a Cujo (Curtis Joseph) fan, especially when he was in Edmonton and I got to go see quite a few Oilers games when I was with my dad," Cam said.

Having already won a Stanley Cup in 2006, and enduring all the ups and downs that go with a two-month playoff marathon, Cam certainly knows what it takes to win in pressure situations. Perhaps his calm demeanor was, in part, developed by the first really high-stakes hockey he played at the Mac's triple-A midget tournament in Calgary. Playing in that derby is the goal of most young players growing up on Canada's prairies, and it attracts an international field.

"It had teams from the States, teams from Europe, so that was always exciting to make that one," Cam said. "I actually went twice."

While Cam's teams never skated off with a championship, simply making the Mac's tournament was an accomplishment in itself.

"It's a tournament that you've got to earn a spot in," he said. "You had to be good enough to get there in the first place."

There's no denying playing goal is one of the toughest jobs in sports. When the team loses, fingers often get pointed at the masked man. Heck, even when teams win a big game the goalie still ends up buried under a pile of smelly hockey players. How fun does that sound?

But according to Ken, Cam always had the mental maturity to man the nets. And the position only served to accentuate Cam's mental strengths.

"As much as you need your teammates, they can't help you when a guy is on a breakaway," said Ken about playing goal. "It's up to you to step up. You're not allowed to just integrate. You have to excel."

It's safe to say his son has done just that.

★★ TIP   *"People often overlook the fact goalies need to be strong skaters, just like defencemen and forwards. In order to recover quickly and stop second chances, a goalie must be a swift skater."*

– RD

Wojtek
Wolski

Competitive Fire

Born:	Feb. 24, 1986 – Zabrze, Poland
First Team:	West Mall Lightning
Heroes:	Ryan Smyth, Sergei Fedorov, Peter Forsberg
NHL Debut:	Oct. 5, 2005 at Edmonton

I n Canada, where hockey is sometimes said to be like a religion, Wojtek Wolski combined the two things in a rather unique way to launch a career that would see him eventually reach the NHL.

"I used the money I got for making my First Communion to buy hockey equipment," recalled the Colorado Avalanche left winger.

Wojtek has not lost sight of that solemn occasion at Maximillian Kolbe Church in Mississauga, Ont., but he also cherishes the day he got his first pair of skates. When he was a boy, Wojtek shared a sofa bed and a pair of blades with his brother Kordian, who is five years older.

"My dad got an old pair of beat-up skates," Wojtek said. "There wasn't enough money for another pair. I wore extra pairs of socks so they would fit."

Wojtek was just four years old when he came to Canada with his father Wieslaw (Wes) and mother Zofia from Zabrze, Poland, via Berlin, in the late 1980s. The family arrived with absolutely nothing and lived with an aunt and uncle for months until Wieslaw and Zofia found jobs.

Wojtek started skating at age seven on a tennis court near his home that was transformed into an ice rink during the winter. "The first year I was terrible, then I went for skating lessons," he said.

Wojtek took the first big step in his path to the pros at a Toronto hockey school called 'Sk8On' operated by Jari Byrski, also a native of Poland, who specializes in complex European skating drills to increase speed and agility. Wojtek often spent six hours a day there.

"I learned all the skills at the hockey school and I had a chance to practise with a lot of good players," he said. "I still go to the same school in the summer and work out with guys like Jason Spezza and Manny Malhotra."

Wojtek first played competitively with the West Mall Lightning, a single-A team in Etobicoke, Ont. But Dave Odd, a coach in the Toronto Marlboros organization, had his eye on Wojtek when he was just nine and finally convinced him to play for the Marlboros' minor peewee team when he was 12.

"He was the first coach I had that really paid attention to skills and conditioning," Wojtek said. "We ran hills at Centennial Park in Etobicoke."

And Odd remembers his student just as well.

"If I did anything, I instilled a sense of teamwork in him," Odd said. "He was more of an individual player when he came to us.

"Eighty per cent of our team drills involved the puck, rather than just trying to go around pylons the whole practice. He had to learn to use his teammates around him. The last couple of weeks of August, we sent out mailers to show the kids what they needed to do to get ready for the season."

Odd said Wojtek had that extra bit of determination, right from the first day he saw him.

"He wanted to be the first up the hill and the other kids fed off that," he said.

A year later, in 1999–2000, 13-year-old Wojtek was the star of the Marlboros peewee team, which won the all-Ontario championship. The team went undefeated through the Greater Toronto League regular season. He completely dominated the championship tournament in Sarnia, leading it in scoring and being named MVP.

"That was the top of the hill for him," Odd said. "In the championship game against Oakville, he made their goalies look like real peewees."

After playing Jr. A at St. Mike's in Toronto, Wojtek was selected third overall in the 2002 Ontario League draft by the Brampton Battalion.

At 16, he was the youngest player on the team in his first season, but he made the OHL all-rookie team and proved he could play with guys as much as four years his elder.

Growing up, Wojtek admired the play of hard-working Ryan Smyth. He also idolized Sergei Fedorov and Peter Forsberg, because they both played solid defence, in addition to having great offensive talents.

Although, by North American standards, he was a little late learning to skate, Wojtek does have some great athletic genes. His uncle, Stefan Mila, played pro soccer for the Gwardia Koszalin team in Poland and cousin, Sebastian Mila, has played for the Polish national soccer team. Wojtek, himself, played soccer and roller hockey as a boy, but has mixed feelings about the value of roller hockey as a complement to ice hockey.

"It helps players become more creative," he said. "But it shortens your stride, you're not pushing off like you would in hockey."

His philosophy for training kids is simple. "It's mostly enjoying yourself and having fun," he said. "Make sure they have a focus, and that it stems from having fun. When they get older, about 14 or 15, you can make sure they are working on their skills."

In 2005, Colorado coach Joel Quenneville was immediately impressed by Wojtek's performance in his NHL debut, recording two goals and six points in nine games to start the season, before being returned to Brampton. Colorado had made Wojtek its first round draft selection the summer before.

"He really has quick hands around the net," Quenneville said. "He does a lot of things that you don't see kids that age do. He shows great patience with the puck. He makes plays, sees plays."

In Brampton that season, Wojtek was named OHL player of the year and also most sportsmanlike player. He finished third in the league scoring race with 47 goals and 128 points in just 56 games.

He was recalled for the 2006 NHL playoffs against Dallas and in his first game scored a goal and set up two others in an Avs win.

Wojtek was the youngest player on the Avs' roster in 2006–07, finishing fourth in league-wide rookie scoring with 50 points and fifth in rookie goals with 22. His first pro contract with the Avalanche, worth a little under $1 million, helped his parents afford a new house and his father secure his own contracting company.

"I remember the first time I went back home to my parents' new four-bedroom house in Mississauga," he said. "I knew it wasn't long ago that I shared a sofa bed and a pair of skates with my brother."

There was one major disappointment along the way. In his last year of junior, Wojtek was not invited to Canada's national junior team. That drove him to play better down the stretch in Brampton, but he still aches from the snub.

He speaks perfect Polish and has been invited to play for the Polish national team, but declined because his dream still is to play for Canada in a major international tournament

Wieslaw has taken his family back to the small village in Poland where they were born, and Wojtek appreciates the sacrifices his parents made.

"I'm very proud of my dad and everything he has accomplished," he said. "I love what he has done for the family. He came from a very poor family and he didn't have the opportunities other people have had."

✦ DRILL   *"Pay attention to dry-land training. For example, a lot of one-legged squats and sprints, either up hills on foot or on a bike, are good for developing fast-twitch muscles."*

– Denis Gibbons

The Future
Young Guns

Hockey is a young man's game, which is why you're reading this book. But as soon as one crop of new stars hits its stride, another group is emerging through junior, NCAA, and Europe to challenge it. With that in mind, here's a list of a dozen sure-fire NHL prospects to watch for in the next few years —the future young guns.

Nicklas Backstrom
Washington Capitals

Born: Nov. 23, 1987

Last Developmental Team: Brynas (Sweden)

If there was any question about the accuracy of Nicklas Backstrom's shot, an Internet video that made the rounds last year put it to rest. In the clip, Nicklas can be seen purposely ringing shots off both posts and the crossbar, not missing once. To say the exciting young playmaker knows what he's doing is an understatement.

With dynamic Russian wingers Alex Ovechkin and Alexander Semin already on their roster, the Capitals have no lack of finish. But who is going to set them up? Nicklas will be a big part of the answer.

Drafted fourth overall in 2006 by Washington, the selection of Nicklas was actually announced on stage by Ovechkin, so it's obvious Ovie's a fan.

After an impressive 2005–06 campaign as a 17-year-old, Nicklas decided to stay in Sweden for more seasoning. In 2006–07, he led his club Brynas in scoring with 40 points in 45 games, good for 22nd in the league. He bolted out of the gate and actually led Sweden's top league in scoring early on with eight goals and 20 points through 14 games.

Nicklas is already getting compared to other Swedish greats such as Peter Forsberg and Henrik Zetterberg.

— RK

Erik Johnson

St. Louis Blues

Born: March 21, 1988

Last Developmental Team: University of Minnesota (NCAA)

Erik Johnson knew he had a lot of fans who wanted to see him play. The only problem was, they cheered for two different teams.

Fans of the St. Louis Blues, who had drafted the 6-foot-4, 220-pound prototypical defenceman with the No. 1 overall pick in 2006, were hoping Erik would make the leap from the U.S. national team development program directly to the NHL and relieve some of their team's recent futility. Slightly north of there, the Golden Gophers faithful at the University of Minnesota wanted to see their homegrown star play at Mariucci Arena.

In the end, a compromise: Erik played for the Gophers in 2006–07, eliciting chants of "Three more years!" before the season had even ended, then signed on with the Blues, where he immediately takes on the responsibility of a franchise player.

Mentioned in the same breath as a former towering Blues defender (Chris Pronger), Erik has great offensive skills from the point to go along with size and a remarkable degree of poise for a teenager.

Erik has authored two solid performances at the World Junior Championship, first propelling himself into the consensus No. 1 pick slot in 2006 and then tying for the tournament scoring lead the next year. He was also named top defender at the tourney, a role his fans hope he will assume in St. Louis.

– RK

<mark>Jack</mark> Johnson

L.A. Kings

Born: Jan. 13, 1987

Last Developmental team: Michigan Wolverines (NCAA)

He shares his name with a popular musician and someday he may well have Carolina GM Jim Rutherford singing the blues.

After drafting him third overall in 2005, Rutherford traded Jack Johnson to the L.A. Kings in the summer of 2006. Now, L.A. GM Dean Lombardi hopes the 6-foot-1, 210-pound defenceman will anchor his blueline for years to come.

Jack, a native of Indianapolis, melds size, physicality and offensive ability into one potent package. It's conceivable Jack, who played five games with L.A. at the end of the 2006–07 season, could one day contribute the type of blueline presence Scott Stevens provided for the New Jersey Devils for so many seasons, while quite possibly producing more points. He contributed nearly a point a game over two seasons on the Michigan Wolverines' blueline.

In his second year, Jack set a sophomore record with 16 goals and was named Central Collegiate Hockey Association offensive defenceman of the year. He has twice suited up for Team USA at the World Junior Championship, earning a tournament all-star berth in 2006. Jack has been a good friend of Sidney Crosby since the two were high school teammates at Shattuck-St. Mary's in Minnesota.

– RD

Patrick Kane

Chicago Blackhawks

Born: Nov. 19, 1988

Last Developmental Team: London Knights (OHL)

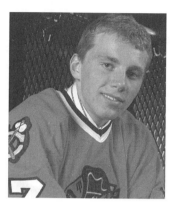

Patrick Kane was a man on the move during the 2006–07 season, his first major junior campaign.

Not only did the Buffalo native make a habit of blowing by opposing defenders, he climbed 35 spots in International Scouting Services draft rankings and eventually went first overall to the Chicago Blackhawks. Patrick inspired Chicago to select him by leading all Ontario League scorers with 62 goals and 145 points as he was named the OHL's rookie of the year.

He's not big (5-foot-9, 160 pounds), but unless the NHL institutes a you-must-be-this-tall-to-play policy, size won't be an issue. Patrick's slick hands have buckled the best defenders and goalies in major junior and there's little doubt his skills and playmaking ability will translate to the big-league level.

Patrick played for Team USA at the 2007 World Junior Championship and finished the event tied for second in tournament scoring, earning him an appointment to the all-star team.

Patrick's first sporting moment in Chicago came when he threw out the first pitch at a Chicago Cubs game shortly after being drafted by the Hawks.

– RD

Kris Letang
Pittsburgh Penguins

Born: April 24, 1987

Last Developmental Team: Val-d'Or (QMJHL)

As if the Pittsburgh Penguins didn't have enough young weapons on their roster, they also have defenceman Kris Letang in the pipeline.

Kris actually started the 2006–07 season with Pittsburgh, notching two goals in seven games before being sent back to junior. The Montreal native was so impressive in training camp that he even surprised himself: Kris didn't pack an autumn jacket when he left for Pittsburgh because he figured he'd be back sooner.

At the time, there were calls for him to remain with the big club, but Kris was returned to the Quebec League. He torched the competition from the blueline, putting up 14 goals and 52 points in just 40 games for Val d'Or.

A smooth skater who likes to push the puck up the ice, Kris also demonstrated his leadership skills in 2007 as captain of Canada's gold-medal-winning entry at the World Junior Championship. At 5-foot-11, he's certainly not a monster defenceman, but he has bulked up considerably since his first year in junior.

Joining a cabal of young talent that includes fellow defenceman Ryan Whitney, goalie Marc-Andre Fleury and forwards Sidney Crosby, Evgeni Malkin and Jordan Staal, Kris adds to the staggering talent the Pittsburgh Penguins have amassed.

– RK

Peter Mueller

Phoenix Coyotes

Born: April 14, 1988

Last Developmental Team: Everett Silvertips (WHL)

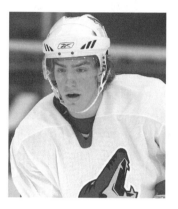

Instincts can't be taught. And when it comes to knowing his way around the offensive zone, Peter Mueller certainly has a great feel for the game.

The 6-foot-2, 205-pound pivot made such an impression on coach Wayne Gretzky at training camp that he very nearly made the Phoenix Coyotes prior to the 2006–07 season. After being sent back down to the Everett Silvertips of the Western League, the Bloomington, Minn. native posted 78 points in 51 games. That marked a 20-point improvement over his first season with the Silvertips, when Peter was named the league's rookie of the year. He's not blessed with exquisite skating ability, but Peter's a crafty player who benefits from already having grown to an imposing frame.

Peter, drafted eighth overall by Phoenix in 2006, didn't put up stunning numbers, but was still a heavy contributor for Team USA at the 2007 World Junior Championship. Peter also donned the stars and stripes at the 2006 world juniors and helped Team USA bag the gold medal at the 2005 under-18 World Championship with seven points in six games.

– RD

▰▰ Carey Price

Montreal Canadiens

Born: Aug. 16, 1987

Last Developmental Team: Tri-City Americans (WHL)

Carey Price's pre-NHL resume is about as decorated as it gets.

The goalie backstopped Canada to gold at the 2007 World Junior Championship, picking up tournament MVP honours along the way. For an encore, Carey led the Hamilton Bulldogs to the Calder Cup later that spring after joining the team when his Tri-City Americans were eliminated from the Western League playoffs. His 2.06 goals-against average and .936 save percentage in the American League playoffs earned Carey his second MVP selection of the season. No wonder the Montreal Canadiens, who drafted Carey fifth overall in the 2005 draft, have such high hopes for him.

Carey brings good size at 6-foot-2 and 175 pounds, and has a hybrid style, mixing elements of the butterfly technique with a more old school stand-up goalie approach. His quick reflexes and solid positioning certainly serve him well, but what really gives Carey such big-game goalie potential is his incredible poise and calm demeanor. When he was growing up in tiny Anahim Lake, B.C., Carey's dad, Jerry, bought a small plane to fly him the 640-kilometre round trip to Williams Lake so he could play minor hockey.

– RD

 Rask

Boston Bruins

Born: March 10, 1987

Last Developmental Team: Ilves (Finland)

Tuukka Rask was still in Finland when he got a pretty good indication of his value: a starting goaltender. That's what the Toronto Maple Leafs acquired from Boston in exchange for the cool Scandinavian netminder back in 2006.

Andrew Raycroft, the goalie in question, had an up-and-down 2006–07 season with the Leafs, while Tuukka stayed in Europe and gave the world a preview of his skill set between the pipes.

Joining a long line of Finnish goaltenders who have dazzled North American crowds (Miikka Kiprusoff, Kari Lehtonen, Nicklas Backstrom), Tuukka's defining career moments to date came at the World Junior Championship in 2006. Taking on arch-rival Sweden in the quarterfinal, Tuukka was peppered with 53 shots and saved each and every one of them. He followed up that stunning performance by staring down Canada in the semifinal in front of a raucous Vancouver crowd. Tuukka did everything he could to keep his Finnish squad in the game, valiantly stopping 39 shots. Canada won the game 4-1, but Rask's performance was well noted.

In 2006–07, Tuukka was called upon to carry his club team Ilves and did so, posting a .928 save percentage while facing the second-most shots in the Finnish League. Not only that, but he also managed to find time to finish his obligatory military service in Finland.

– RK

Marc Staal

New York Rangers

Born: Jan. 13, 1987

Last Developmental Team: Sudbury Wolves (OHL)

His brothers may have blazed the path, but there's little doubt Marc Staal is going to carve out a reputation of his own as a tremendous NHL player.

A couple of things separate Marc from his brothers Eric and Jordan. First, there's the fact he's a defenceman, not a forward. Secondly, Marc plays with a nastier edge than either of the other two Staal boys currently in the NHL. Marc's game is not about putting points on the board, but rather keeping opposing attackers in check with his toughness and mobility. He willed Sudbury to the 2007 Ontario League final with his rugged play and shutdown capabilities. Despite the fact the Wolves lost the final to the Plymouth Whalers, Marc's incredible play was recognized with playoff MVP honours. He was also a standout defenceman on Canadian teams that won gold at the World Junior Championship in 2006 and 2007.

He is the kind of blueliner who figures to see the other team's top players (which will surely include some fierce family battles) for the next decade.

– RD

John Tavares

Eligible for 2009 draft

Born: Sept. 20, 1990

Last Developmental Team: Oshawa Generals (OHL)

John Tavares is a prime example of substance over style.

He'll never overwhelm anybody with blazing speed, but the guy simply knows how to score. He broke Wayne Gretzky's Ontario League record for goals by a 16-year-old during the 2006–07 season with 72—Gretzky had 70—en route to winning league MVP honours. Prior to that, he scored 91 goals as a 14-year-old triple-A midget player with the Toronto Marlboros.

The 6-foot, 183-pound centre has tremendous vision and hockey sense, but perhaps his best attribute is his desire to improve. He's the latest in a line of Oshawa phenoms that includes Bobby Orr and Eric Lindros.

In addition to fighting through checkers, John has also proven he's capable of dealing with the ever-increasing media attention a teenager with his talent attracts. The Oakville, Ont. native was literally tabbed an exceptional player at 15, which allowed him to play major junior one year early. He scored 45 goals and 77 points in his freshman season, taking Canadian League rookie-of-the-year honours.

John was born five days too late to be eligible for the 2008 draft, so he won't be selected by an NHL team until 2009.

— RD

Jonathan Toews

Chicago Blackhawks

Born: April 29, 1988

Last Developmental Team: University of North Dakota (NCAA)

The opportunity to be known as a clutch player was there and Jonathan Toews took it.

The situation was the 2007 World Junior Championship and a berth in the final was on the line. Jonathan and Team Canada were locked in a classic semifinal battle with the United States and everything came down to a shootout. With players allowed to shoot more than once, Jonathan ended up with three chances. He put in all three, including the game winner, past U.S. goalie Jeff Frazee, who had been nearly unbeatable in international play.

Now, Jonathan has his sights set on the NHL.

As one of several blue-chippers ready to burst out in Chicago, Jonathan has been lauded for his leadership and two-way game. He was the only non-NHLer to play for Canada's entry in the 2007 World Championship and did not look out of place. The Manitoba native eschewed Canadian junior hockey in favour of the NCAA and put together two solid seasons at perennial powerhouse North Dakota, where he scored at nearly a point-per-game pace. Before that, he was a standout at Shattuck-St. Mary's, the same Minnesota prep school that had Sidney Crosby and Zach Parise walking through its halls. Don't be surprised to see a 'C' on Jonathan's sweater in the future.

— RK

Kyle Turris

Phoenix Coyotes

Born: Aug. 14, 1989

Last Developmental Team: Burnaby Express (BCHL Jr. A)

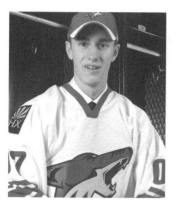

For Kyle Turris, 'Express' isn't just the name of the Jr. A team he played for, it's the speed with which he has arrived in the hockey world.

Kyle, taken with the third pick in the 2007 draft by the Phoenix Coyotes, saw his stock increase by leaps and bounds as the 2006–07 season progressed, peaking at just the right time despite playing against less-than-formidable competition.

Some say he reminds them of Joe Sakic, while others look at his 1-on-1 offensive wizardry and think of Marian Gaborik.

Coyotes coach Wayne Gretzky has been very vocal in his praise for young Kyle. The Great One lauded the teen's speed and attitude and said he couldn't wait to get him in a Phoenix jersey for good.

Before that happens, however, Kyle is headed to the University of Wisconsin.

Being a Badger was so important to the B.C. native that he turned down a chance to play for the Western League's Vancouver Giants in order to maintain his NCAA eligibility.

Not only were the Giants guaranteed a berth in the 2007 Memorial Cup by virtue of being the hosts, but their powerhouse lineup ended up winning the prestigious tournament.

— RK